Boots anc

LIFE AS A RECRUIT IN THE SCOTS GUARDS

Howard Gee

Howard Gee was born and educated in Edinburgh and has worked, travelled and lived throughout Europe and the Far East with his family. Howard is married to Carmine and they have two grown up children and four Grandchildren who are now all very happy to be living in the shadows of the Wallace Monument near Stirling and the magnificent Ochil Hills.

Whilst serving in the Scots Guards, Howard was selected into the Army Physical Training Corps and was involved on active service with the Brigade of Gurkhas in Borneo and with other regiments throughout troubled areas of the world. He served in all Non Commissioned Ranks including Regimental Sergeant Major and was commissioned into the APTC in 1980. He is now retired and writing his memoires; the first of which is titled 'We Were Only Bairns'. The follow-up book 'Boots and Bearskins' is a riotously funny story of army life. Both books let the reader glimpse another world as truth mingles with humour.

To Jackie, Andrew and Alison for their encouragement and support throughout.

Table of Contents

Preface

For a young 17 year old boy, the thought of recruitment into the Scots Guards for three years prior to joining the Edinburgh City Police was an exciting prospect but their renowned discipline was daunting and I was not sure that I was up to the required standard. After some deep consideration, on the 11th June 1959, I took the Oath to Her Majesty the Queen and went through the gates of the Guards depot at Caterham, and entered a world of drill parades, discipline and military humour.

Howard James Grant Gee.

Chapter 1 - The Queen's Shilling

As I stepped through the large iron gates, I saw the sign written in bold letters, 'New Recruits'. 'That's me,' I thought to myself and as I gripped my small suitcase tight, I plucked up courage to go forwards but it was then that I heard the voice shout out, 'What's your name?'

My immediate reaction was to ask, 'Why?' but I didn't. I put my suitcase down and looked up at a giant of a man dressed in army uniform, with a red sash across his chest and three stripes on his arm.

'What's your name boy and where are you from?' he screamed at me again; his lips moving up and down beneath a large fiery red, bushy moustache. I couldn't see his eyes for the peak of his hat which was pulled down on to the bridge of his nose; it had a red and white diced band around it and three gold bands on the peak. Somehow I knew not to get smart with him.

'Howard Gee from Edinburgh,' I said anxious to please. My eyes were transfixed on the razor sharp creases which ran down the front of his trousers, tucking into his black gleaming leather boots via buckled green gaiters around his ankles.

'You call me sergeant when you speak to me,' he bawled

'Yes sergeant,' I tried to shout back but it was a squeaky little sound that came out.

'Don't worry son,' he said in a strong Scottish accent; 'You'll get the hang of it but better make it quick. Runner!!' he shouted.

A soldier came running out of the guardroom trying to press his hat down on to his head whilst stopping himself from tripping over his own feet and almost falling flat on his face. I turned my head to watch him as he took off marching, almost running with his arms swinging backwards and forwards at shoulder height, down the long tree lined avenue stretching from the guardroom. He went like a hare out of the trap; past an enormous square on the left, heading towards some buildings in the distance.

'Follow that man,' shouted the sergeant, 'and don't lose him or you'll be back here spending the night in one of my cells.'

I glanced at the nearby sentry who also had the red and white dicing of the Scots Guards around his hat and was marching up and down outside his sentry box with his rifle tucked into his side looking immediately to his front and ignoring all that was going on. I glanced down at my suitcase resting on the ground, picked it up, looked at the sergeant again and took off after the Runner; I found out later that was what he was officially called.

'Keep behind me,' said the Runner; shouting over his shoulder without turning around. 'Don't dare pass me or I'll be locked up in the guardroom to-night.'

'Aye right', I mumbled to myself as if there was any chance of me even keeping up with him never mind passing him. Out of the corner of my left eye, I could see lots of soldiers marching up and down and around the square, and more soldiers with sticks under their arms shouting and bawling instructions.

The Runner turned right, took a left by a large building with a sign reading NAAFI and swung left again around a corner. Trying to catch my breath and keep hold of my case, I followed on hoping that he wasn't heading out the back door and down the hill to the railway station.

'Are we there yet?' I asked, wishing that I had some knowledge of where our destination was to be.

'We are there,' the Runner said coming to a halt and gulping fresh air into his lungs. This is the Receiving Room where all new recruits report to.

'Is this your full time job in the army?' I asked.

'Just today, while my squad is on guard duty,' he answered. 'We are based in the guardroom and change responsibilities around from being the Runner, collecting

8

meals for the guard, sentry duties, to cleaning our personal kit over a 24hour period. Good luck.' He opened his mouth and gulped in more air as he turned about and was off on the return journey back to the guardroom.

I suddenly felt very alone looking up at the windows of a tall building with the words Receiving Room engraved above the front door. 'What kind of a name was that anyway?' I mumbled to myself. 'I hope I'm not sleeping here on my own. What if the place is haunted? Have I done the right thing leaving my warm cosy bed in Edinburgh?'

I had yearned at the tender age of seventeen and a half years to have some excitement in my life and on the 11th of June 1959, so I reported to the Army Recruiting Office in Queensferry Road, Edinburgh to take the Queen's Shilling. With my right hand on the bible, I took the Oath of Allegiance to Her Majesty the Queen and joined the Scots Guards. That evening I said farewell to Carmine my girlfriend and all the family who came to wave me off at the Waverly Station.

I had taken the ten o'clock overnight train from Edinburgh to Kings Cross, and on arrival, crossed by taxi to London Bridge Station and onwards to Caterham in Surrey. I had caught the first bus up the hill to the Guards Depot and when I asked the bus driver if he would please let me off at the correct gates. His reply was that the Surrey Mental Institution was next door to The Guards Depot but in spite of the very high surrounding wall, it didn't really matter which gates I went through, I would end up in the same place. I wasn't quite sure what he meant.

Chapter 2 - A Raw Recruit

Just grab any bed, said a lad with a Welsh accent. I'm Dai Roberts and I'm joining the Welsh Guards.

'Oh, sorry! Am I in the wrong room?' I asked.

'No, no boyo,' he replied. 'We are all joining different regiments from the five Regiments of Foot guards. We have been given a paper to study their histories. I'll give you them in regimental seniority starting with the Grenadiers, followed by the Coldstreams, the Scots Guards, followed by the Irish and bravest of all, the youngest and best regiment, the Welsh Guards. Judging by your accent you must be joining the Third regiment of Foot Guards, the Scots Guards raised in 1642. No you're in the correct barrack room, right enough. Weren't you lucky to beat us at Murrayfield last week?'

With my suitcase still in my hand, I was trying to collect my thoughts and was about to reply, that we were worthy winners of the rugby match but before I could open my mouth, I was surrounded by a crowd of smiling friendly faces and jostling bodies all trying to shake my hand and introduce themselves and tell me what regiment they were joining.

'What's your name?' someone asked.

'It's Howard and I'm from Edinburgh. When did you all arrive?'

'Over the last three days,' came the reply in an Irish accent

A tall lad stepped forward; I'm Murdoch MacLeod from Inverness. Since I arrived first I was nominated by the Receiving Room Sergeant to show new arrivals the ropes;how to make up their beds, collect their kfs and mug from the storeroom on the landing, ready for dinner at 1230. We all have to go over together to the cookhouse, walking quickly with your left hand behind your back holding your kfs and mug; your right hand swings forward and backwards. Hands in pockets are definitely a big no.'

'What's kfs?' I asked cautiously in case it was obvious and I should have known.

'Knife, fork and spoon,' came the loud response from all around me who had been waiting for me to ask the question.

'Don't worry,' said Murdoch, 'we all fell for that one. Come on over to your bed space and I'll show you how to make it, and give you some notes of information to read up on. The Sergeant will be coming round at 4pm for roll call before tea. You'll hear him before he steps in through the door.

'Does he wear tackity boots?' I asked

'He does, but you'll hear him before he even puts his feet on the stairs,' replied Murdoch. 'I think there is still a few to arrive throughout today. Tomorrow we leave here and disperse to our own regimental lines. Don't worry, Howard, I'll keep you right, we'll be Scots Guards together.'

'Thanks ,' I said and made my way over to an iron bed with a white thick mattress cover lying folded with three blankets, two sheets, a pillow and a pillow case on top of a straw mattress.

Murdoch proceeded to show me how to make my bed, army style. Mattress cover on first, followed by the sheets and blankets; fold the blankets down at the sides and tuck them under the mattress 'like they do in the hospital,' he said. I was shown the large cupboard where the brooms, shovels, dusters, bluebell for the brasses, scrubbing brushes and mops were kept, and the star of the cleaning materials, the bumper. This was a rectangular type of mop which weighed a ton to lift and had a very long handle that allowed two people to hold it simultaneously while swinging backwards and forwards along the brown coloured linoleum. The thick polish, which was rubbed into the linoleum and left to penetrate overnight, was bumpered up after breakfast, leaving the floor gleaming for the room inspection along with the toilets, showers, baths, sinks, wash hand basins and door handles, not to mention lockers (inside, outside and on top), windowsills, under beds, tops of doors and all ledges that could possibly harbour a spot of dust.

'I suppose you used one at home,' said Jacob who was about to join the Coldstream Guards.

'One what?' I asked.

'A bumper,'

I looked at him in amazement, shaking my head. He smiled, 'just joking,' he said.

The rest of the morning passed very quickly and I was feeling hungry and ready for dinner when Murdoch shouted, 'it's twenty five past, everyone outside and get in three lines. No mucking about now and remember to take your mug and cutlery.' We formed up under Murdoch's guidance and walked around to the cookhouse to join the queue of recruits who appeared from all over the barracks.

'Just arrived?' asked a lad in a broad Irish accent wearing denims and an Irish Guards badge in his beret.

'This morning,' I said.

'It will all seem a bit strange to you but to be sure you'll get the hang of things quickly,' he said.

'Aye mun, better be very quickly, or life will be a real misery. I'm Kelvin Brown nicknamed Bomber. I'm Grenadiers and my squad is in their third week of training.'

'How many weeks do you train for?' I asked trying to seem intelligent.

Twelve weeks training, here at Caterham and six weeks at the Training Battalion at Pirbright where we do shooting on the ranges and night exercises before we join our battalions. It could all be longer if the squad fail the Inspection before their Passing Out Parade or if you are back squaded for not being up to standard with the cleaning of your kit, squad marching or if you've been sick and required medical treatment.

'What sort of medical treatment?' I asked getting rather concerned

12

'Well if you fall off the wall on the assault course or the death slide you could easily break a leg.'

'Death slide?' I asked. Had I heard right? 'What's that?'

'Or twist your shoulder on the high nets or even panic and jar your neck in the underground tunnels,' said a voice with a Welsh accent behind me, ignoring my question. I nearly got bitten by that dragon that lives down there the other day.

Roars of laughter broke out. 'Not even a hungry dragon would eat you Taffy;' came a voice from the front of the queue, 'wouldn't risk indigestion.' The sounds of the cookhouse doors being opened brought the frivolity to an end and the long queue started to move inside, controlled by the duty Lance Corporal wearing a white band around his hat denoting a member of the Coldstream Guards.

'He has two stripes on his arm Murdoch, why is he called Lance Corporal?' I asked, knowing that a Corporal had two stripes. .

'Very observant Howard, only in the Guards does a Lance Corporal have two stripes and a Lance Sergeant three. It goes back to the time that Queen Victoria was taking the salute on parade and she couldn't visibly make out the badges of rank on the arms of the Junior Non Commissioned Officers and from that day onwards the matter was solved.'

'Well how do you know a L/Sgt from a full Sergeant?' I asked.

'Well they both shout at you but the sergeant shouts louder, wears a red sash, has three gold bands on the peak of his hat, has a slightly different cap badge and carries a pace stick. Don't ask, you'll find out about a pace stick later. Oh and by the way don't worry about the death slide, we'll be on it soon enough; a bit of daring fun, I've been told as long as you hang on.'

'Come on keep moving,' shouted someone from the rear of the queue. We're back on parade at 1330 hours.

We collected our plates and moved forwards with the queue to where the cooks were standing in a row along the back of the hotplates, watching the hungry recruits fill their plates with the freshly cooked food laid out in trays. I had never seen such amounts of food at dinner time and when I saw the crisp brown chips inviting me to try one, I did. I didn't see the deft flick of the long handled metal spoon but felt the sharp pain as it landed on the back of my hand. 'Ouch!!' I shouted and looked up at a tall figure wearing blue and white checked trousers, a white jacket, a red and blue Brigade of Guards tie and a forage cap with red and white dicing. He had three stripes and a crown on his arm and I knew that he was important.

'You'll no dae that again laddie,' he said glowering at me. Help yourself to as much food as you like but put it on your plate and take it back to your table before you start eating it. 'Do you understand me?'

'Yes sir,' I shouted out; the standard reply.

'Is that a Scots accent I'm hearing?' asked the Colour Sergeant and where are you from?'

'Edinburgh,' I answered resisting rubbing my knuckle whilst trying to hold back a tear from rolling out of my eye.

'Well,' he said with a change of tone in his voice. 'How's auld Reekie?'

'Fine sir.' I said

'Yer going tae a fine regiment, the best,' he said. 'Just you relax, enjoy yourself and remember what I told you.'

'I will sir,' I said moving along the hotplate to the puddings and glancing down at my throbbing knuckle of my right hand.

'I bet you felt that,' said Murdoch grinning.

'Na,' I lied.

After dinner we were allowed to make our way back to the Receiving Room in pairs or small groups, not sauntering but moving quickly with our clean eating irons and mug which we had washed at the large sinks situated outside the cookhouse.

After dinner new cleaning tasks were again listed on the notice board and were carried out as a team whilst talking and laughing throughout the afternoon. We waited in trepidation for the entrance of the Recruiting Sergeant at 1600 hours.

Chapter 3 - The Army Way

'Stand by your beds,' the words reverberated up the stairs and into the room. All activity stopped and everyone stood to attention at the end of their beds, looking straight ahead at the man opposite.

The sergeant stooped and just managed to keep his hat on as he stepped through the door. 'Stand still and look to your front,' he ordered with a commanding power from his vocal cords. 'MacLeod, I see that we have a few new members, the bed spaces are filling up. Have you got the millboard with the names and regiments of choice?'

'Yes Sergeant,' replied Murdoch as he handed over the nominal roll.

'Good afternoon gentlemen.' The sergeant said with a hint of sarcasm in the tone of his voice.

'Good afternoon Sergeant,' we responded; just like being back at school, I thought to myself.

'That will probably be the last time you will be called gentlemen he said. As from tomorrow after breakfast, you will be joining your training squads of your individual regiments and you might even be called Guardsman. My name is Sergeant Evans and you will call me, Sergeant Evans. I see that there are five of you joining my own regiment, the Welsh Guards. When you are issued with your army number, the last three digits will be used after your surname to distinguish which Jones or Davies you are. You see there are so many of us Welshmen with the same name and before you even think it, no we didn't have the same father,' he said looking around daring anyone to even raise their eyebrows in disbelief..

Tonight is your last night in the same group; so if you want to enjoy a pint of beer together in the NAAFI this evening, make the most of it but do not, and I repeat, do not have too much to drink as tomorrow from reveille your feet won't be touching the ground.

You will have realised by now that at 0600 hours, a bugle call wakens everyone up except the Jocks who awaken a few seconds later when their bagpipes go off. When you hear the call leap out of bed, get washed, shaved, dressed, and march at a fast rate of knots down to the cookhouse for breakfast and be back outside in three ranks by 0730 hours. Before that time, you will have scrubbed out the latrines, cleaned out the wash hand basins, showers and baths, polished the floor, made up your beds, dusted your lockers and completed all the other tasks already allotted to you. Make sure that you are up to scratch with your regimental histories as your Squad Sergeants will be testing you when they arrive tomorrow morning. They will be marching you over to the Quarter Master's Store for the issue of all your kit. Any questions boyo's?'

'Yes Sergeant,' I said.

'Well what is it? I haven't got all day to spend talking to a wild Highland tribesman from Scotland.'

'What does the wee tree in your hat represent sergeant?'

'Wee tree?' What wee tree?'

The one you wear as a cap badge.'

There was a deathly hush and I could feel everyone's eyes trying to look sideways at me without moving their heads.

Sergeant Evans went scarlet, threw his pace stick on to the floor and looked at me as if he was some monster who had just climbed out of the Welsh coalmines and was about to devour me and spit out the bones, assuming that there was anything left.

'Are you winding me up boyo?' he asked

'No sergeant,' I replied now realising and regretting that I had said something that had upset him.

'The Welsh Guard's cap badge is a leek, not a wee tree but a Welsh leek; grown in our greenest Welsh valleys.'

'Oh! sorry sergeant, I see it now,'

Sergeant Evans, picked up his pace stick, made some comment about where he would like to shove it, pulled his jacket down under his belt, adjusted his hat and stormed out of the room.

Once the room was certain that he had left the building, everyone, relaxed and burst into fits of laughter even the Welsh lads thought it was funny.

'A good question,' said Murdoch.

'I don't think Sergeant Evans has a sense of humour,' said Mel Griffiths who was himself from the valleys; after all how would a jock be expected to know what a leek looked like; now if it had been a haggis,'

'What's a haggis?' asked Willie MacFarlane from Belfast.

'That's the wee creatures in Scotland that are fed on shamrocks to make them big and strong' answered Tom Seivright. Why don't all the regiments have a cap badge like ours which is easily identified, like a grenade representing the Grenadier Guards?

'I thought that was an exploding balloon', answered Wilfred Blackwood from Bolton who was following his father's footsteps into the Coldstream Guards. Laughter broke out from around the room. He didn't see the pillow winging its way towards him.

'It's alright having a laugh between ourselves but regiments and traditions are taken very seriously in the Brigade of Guards Howard,' said Rab MacAlistair, a Scots lad from Troon in Ayrshire, 'and everyone is very proud and a wee bit touchy about their own regimental uniforms, badges and traditions. Right! Howard,' he said, 'you have been here a few hours now so I'm going to test you. What's the Scots Guards Motto as shown on our cap badge?'

'Never wear underpants under your kilt,' I replied quickly,

Quick answer but wrong Howard,' he said, laughing out loud. It's 'Nemo Me Impune Lacessit' which means, but before he could answer I said, 'Touch Me Not With Impunity,'

Rab's mouth opened in amazement. 'Well done Howard, you've been studying our Regimental History paper. You can help me with mine. I can never remember dates and things like that.'

'Did you not do history at school?' I asked.

'Well we didn't do too much of it at borstal,' he replied

'Oh,' I said, glad to be distracted with Murdoch slapping me on the back.

'That's braw Howard. Well done.'

'Och, it was nothing,' I replied.

'Right lads,' shouted Murdoch, 'let's get any letters for home finished and get over to the cookhouse for tea. Any shoes to be cleaned, washing or ironing can be done with other personal chores before we all go down to the NAFFI for a few beers tonight. Sean O Hara Irish Guards has agreed to buy the first round.'

'Well done Sean,' shouted Mathew Boland another potential Grenadier Recruit. 'A big cheer lads for Sean,'

'To be sure; what did Murdoch say?' asked Sean.

'Oh not to worry Sean,' Michael Rafferty answered, 'the English Grenadier lads are going to pay for the first round,'

'Well,' said Sean, 'I would never have thought that of the English. God bless you lads.'

The NAFFI was packed with recruits who were in various weeks of training and after a few beers, some jokes and stories, a night full of banter, even a few rowdy songs and lots of laughter, we made our way back to the room, showered and headed for bed apprehensive of the following morning and aware that we were all going different ways to our chosen regiments within different areas of the camp.

Chapter 4 - Kitted Out

At 0720 hours sharp, the whole Receiving Room emptied and all the new recruits stood outside awaiting the appearance of their Regimental Squad Sergeants who duly appeared at 0729 hours and introduced themselves prior to organising their own regimental recruits into their Training Squads. When Lance Sergeant Bath, stepped forward, he was probably the smartest man I had ever seen. His boots were gleaming in the morning sunshine, the creases in his battledress trousers and on the arms of his jacket were razor sharp and his white buff belt around his waist linked the two together as if he was wearing a one piece suit tailor made specifically for him. The flaps of his jacket pockets were pressed down on to his chest and the knot of his tie wedged neatly into his immaculately ironed shirt collar. With his chin held up to permit his eyes to see from under the peak of his hat, his military cane was tucked under his left arm and held in place by his left hand which allowed him to salute the officer hovering in the background with his right hand. He was immaculate and his whole body posture represented the words carried on the blue tab sewn on to both shoulders at the top of the sleeves which read Scots Guards.

Each of the regimental squads were now being addressed and briefed by their squad Lance Sergeants. They were telling them that they had been allocated various times for marching around the camp and being introduced to the Medical Officer for a further body inspection, the gymnasium, assault course, their own regimental PT staff and the barber who would dispose of their long flowing locks in less than 1 minute. They would be shown the NAAFI shop where they would be able to buy the required accessories like blanco for their issued webbing, extra bootlaces, padlock and key for their lockers, bluebell with standard yellow dusters for cleaning and polishing, tins of boot polish, stamps for letters home to their mums to tell them how badly they were being treated and maybe a Kit Kat or Mars bar to nibble away at under the blankets after lights out.

Our squad was informed that en route to the Quartermaster's store for the issue of uniforms, kit and equipment we would pass the guardroom. It was emphasised in no uncertain terms that we would spend time in the cold, bleak, miserable cells hanging on to the bars should we have any ideas of disobeying orders from the regimental staff or going absent without leave.

'Don't even think about catching the train home to mummy,' said Sergeant Bath.

'No Sergeant,' we replied.

'Any mental or physical problems that may arise, you will direct to me through your Trained Soldier who is standing on my right,' he continued. His name is Trained Soldier Woods and the regimental star on his right arm means that you will obey his commands without question with speed and willingness. He has been through training, experienced life in the battalion and has been selected to guide and help you through your training. He will be with you throughout each day and night; sleeping in his own bunk next door to your allocated barrack room. You will not even be able to go to the toilet without his permission. Your allocated barrack room will not be ready for a few days yet as the squad currently in it has failed their Passing Out Parade and has been back squaded. That means they are not going on leave as planned and will now be late in going onwards to the Training Battalion at Pirbright for their final six weeks of battle training. They will be inspected again and they had better pass or the wrath of the gods will descend upon them from a great height, and believe me, that isn't something you would want to experience. Until then, you will be accommodated in the wooden huts just behind K. Company Scots Guards from where your training will commence.'

'There are seventeen of you in the squad and from now on you will work as a team and wear the Scots Guard's badge with pride. You are now going to march to the barber shop where you will wait outside until called in by the barber Lance Corporal Jones Welsh Guards or his assistant, Guardsman MacPhee Scots Guards; after which we will cross to the gymnasium to meet your PT Instructors. From there, it's down to the stores for the issuing of kit. Throughout your tour of the depot, you will march with pride, look to your front, head up, no talking and don't even think of laughing, smiling or waving. Trained Soldier Woods will be in charge of you and do not let me down.'

'Do you understand me?'

'Yes Sergeant,' was the unanimous response.

'Let's get cracking then. I will see you later this morning when you have collected your mattresses, bedding and all your kit from the stores, cleaned out your lockers and swept your bed spaces before lunch break at 1230 hours. Take over Trained Soldier.'

'Yes Sergeant. Right you lot, face that way,' shouted the Trained Soldier pointing in what we presumed was the direction of the barbers shop. 'I will call out the time of the steps. Ensure that your arm swinging shoulder high is the opposite of the leg moving forward.' Everyone glanced at each other seeking mental guidance as to what that instruction meant. 'Look to your front,' shouted the Trained Soldier. 'Can you not understand the Queen's English?' Even Hamish MacPherson from South Uist didn't make any comment about understanding the Gaelic better. 'Macleod you are in the front file on the right and everyone will take their step from you.'

'Yes Sergeant,' Murdoch replied proud to be chosen while everyone else was trying to be inconspicuous in the middle of the squad.

Without looking around, everyone heard the long sigh from the Trained Soldier followed by a deep intake of air before the orders rolled out of his mouth. Left foot first; by the right, quick march.' and we were off to meet the staff in the barber's shop.

'Head up, arms shoulder high, left, right, left, right;' all was going well until we reached the road junction and the order 'left wheel,' was called.

'What did he say?' asked someone from the rear rank. Everyone was trying to check with the man next to him before turning the wrong way, but too late. Some of the squad went left, some stood still, others bumped into them and the remainder went right and when the instruction to halt came, everyone just froze in the middle of the road. Trained Soldier Woods went berserk, red faced screaming and shouting trying to herd us into one group again. The tension of the situation arose as the newly formed squad of the Grenadier Guards marched past in perfect disciplined order, encouraged by their squad sergeant to make sheep like noises such as 'baa! baaa!'

After much cursing, swearing, and abusive body language, the Trained Soldier formed us up and marched us on to the barbers. Standing at ease outside waiting to be called in to the shop, there was a distinct feeling of apprehension which grew into silent horror as those who came out were seen trying to feel for hair at the back of their necks but were having to move their hands over the shaven plateau almost to the top of their heads.

'Oh no.' or even more expletive words were heard as individuals stepped out of the shop into full view of those waiting to go in.

'Did you get an anaesthetic?' asked someone in the centre rank which initiated an outbreak of laughter; even Trained Soldier Woods smiled before shouting, 'Keep quiet and look to your front.'

When the last member of the squad had been sheared, we were called to attention by the Trained Soldier. 'I wonder what your mothers would think of their little darlings now. No curly locks to twirl around their little fingers as they hum a lullaby sending you to sleep,' he said, with a sneer glaring at his squad like an evil sorcerer looking into his bubbling cauldron; wringing his hands and casting his spell..

'Stand to attention you shower of useless perverts. Listen to my commands. I repeat listen to my commands and obey them correctly. Right turn,' he said slowly; 'Quick march, left, right, left, right,' he called out and the whole squad moved forwards.

The command of 'right wheel,' rang out and the squad moved as one body to the right and the gymnasium came into sight. Not a word was said but a feeling of pride crept through the squad and from my position in the rear I could see heads being lifted just a little bit higher.

Before reaching the gymnasium, we were brought to a halt at the assault course where we stood in amazement as a squad of Coldstream Guards were climbing up and rolling over the log at the top of a very tall net hanging between two large trees. On scrambling down the other side of the net, they had to grab hold of one of three available ropes and swing across a large ditch full of water; jumping off the rope when reaching the far bank. Most never reached the bank but went crashing into the water when the instructors bawled at them to get their lazy arses out and try again.

'That looks good fun,' I said

'Looks pretty difficult to me,' replied Ewan Stuart

'Don't forget that they are Coldstreams,' commented Trained Soldier Woods. 'Everything is difficult for them.' The whole squad burst out laughing.

'Well!' said a voice at the rear of the squad, 'I'll expect better from you when it's your turn. I'm Lance Sergeant Park, Scots Guards, your PT instructor. That's the gymnasium behind me,' he said pointing in the direction of a large building and I'll be seeing you there within a few days.'

'Where is your next stop Trained Soldier?' he asked

'Medical Officer and the Quartermaster's store, Sergeant,' he replied.

'Well don't be late and I'll look forward to seeing this new squad when they come to the gymnasium.'

Down to the medical centre we were marched, where the Medical Officer reminded us that, we had already passed our initial medical examination prior to travelling to the Depot but that we would now be examined again and have our bodies confirmed as healthy or otherwise.

'If you would be kind enough to strip off and stand in a straight line, I'll inspect each of you individually.' he said. He walked along the line looking into our eyes, ears and mouths; held a stethoscope to our chest and his hand under our testicles asking us to cough; what that was supposed to tell him about us, I'm not sure but he had a smile on his face as he moved down the line and around the back. 'Now,' he said, 'let's see you all bend down and touch your toes and hold that position until I say up, and no comments please. That looks good. A fine body of men indeed. Right gentlemen, stand up and get dressed.'

'Now,' he continued, 'is there is anyone feeling unwell or sick at this moment? Homesick doesn't count nor does feeling sad or down in the dumps; they are all pretty normal symptoms here at the Depot. I've no doubt I will be seeing you with minor scrapes and bruises once your training gets underway although I've always found the Scots to be a hardy bunch; it must be the weather up there. Any malingerers will be dealt with quickly and no mercy shown,' he said, 'and as for healthy minds, I'll leave that to the Padre to sort out.'

As we passed the NAAFI shop we kept marching and the Trained Soldier pointed out that we could buy anything we needed on our way back to the barrack room after lunch.

We stood at ease outside the Quartermaster's store, until we were introduced to Company Quarter Master Sergeant Humphries who had three stripes and a crown. The red colour around his forage cap and the little bomb thing for his cap badge informed us that he was in the Grenadier Guards.

'You will be pleased to hear that your mattresses and covers have already been delivered to your company lines. We in the Grenadiers know that you Jocks would be struggling to carry them, would probably lay them down for a rest and would then fall asleep on them before you reached your barrack room which would be completely unacceptable. We do have however, ready and waiting for you to collect, upon receipt of your signature, three blankets, two sheets and one pillow with pillow case white. Hot water bottles are not supplied and oh! don't you even dare to think of sleeping on your mattress without putting the mattress cover on first. Do you all understand me?'

'Yes,--------'. There was a deathly hush as no one was sure what a sergeant with a crown was called.

'You can call me sir,' he said quietly as he smiled and pointed to the open door of the stores. 'Lead on one at a time.'

How we ever made it to K Company Lines in any semblance of order, trying to look over the top of our pile of bedding, I'll never know but it was largely due to the Trained Soldier's skill in herding us together and to everyone else in the Depot keeping out of our way.

'When you get to the barrack room, select the beds to your left and right as you enter,' was the instruction shouted out. 'Help each other to put the mattress cover on, make up your beds and then form up outside to return to the stores for the issuing of kit. The room key will be retained by Scott and don't lose it.'

Back at the Quartermaster's store we formed a queue and followed the man in front, in through the double doors to face the longest counter I had ever seen, and as ordered we moved along it until the first eight of the squad were inside. We each stood in front of individual piles of clothing and equipment already laid out on the counter and the Company Quarter Master Sergeant then started reading out a list of items which we were to mentally check off as present.

'Battledress jacket and trousers,' he called, 'shirts khaki 3, tie, pairs of socks gray 4, under vests white 3, drawers cellular 4, braces 1 pair, brushes small various, vests physical training 1 red, 1 white, shorts 2 pair, plimsolls physical training 1 pair, beret dark blue 1, cap comforter, forage cap with dicing 1.

'Place the forage cap on your head now and my three store assistants will come round and check that you are wearing the correct size. Stand still, head up and shoulders back.' He shouted. Some hats that were too big had fallen down on to the ears of the wearer whilst others were being forced down over their foreheads by the assistants. 'What size of hat do you wear? ' I was asked.

'Is this a trick question?' I asked myself. The only hat I had ever worn was a woolly balaclava knitted by my auntie Annie to keep out the cold Edinburgh winds.

'This seems to fit you quite well,' said the assistant; it will slacken off a bit once it's been worn a while. From now on just remember that you take a size 6&7/8.'

'Yes sir, I will,' remembering to call him sir; if ever in doubt say sir, I had told myself.

'Cap badges Scots Guards 2, kfs sets 1, mess tins 2, mug 1, plates 2, groundsheet, kitbag, towels army white 2, pullover khaki 1, pyjamas pairs 2, housewife; no cracks please,' said the CQMS , 'I've heard them all before. Your housewife will hold, needles large 1, small 2, thread bobbin khaki 1, buttons brown various sizes for sewing and wool gray for socks darning. Denims fatigue jacket and trousers with exchangeable buttons, gloves woollen 1 pair,' he continued. 'respirator and steel helmet with camouflage net , rifle strap, pull through with oil bottle for cleaning of rifle, waist belt webbing 1, with brasses 4, gaiters left & right, large pack, small pack, ammunition pouches 2; all with required shoulder straps. Your bayonet frog is included now but your bayonet and sheath will be issued later in training when you start carrying a rifle. Your belt and gaiters are required to be blancoed and brasses cleaned,' he bellowed, 'so don't plan on going out drinking or to the dancing tonight.'

'Of course not.' I thought to myself, looking around quickly to ensure that no one even suspected what I was thinking.

'You will of course, all be sharing in the costs of buying an iron from the NAAFI for the squad,' said the Company Quarter Master Sergeant. 'Your trousers and jacket will require pressing and shirts ironed immediately. All creases will be immaculate which I know your Trained Soldier will ensure. Behind you is a bench on which you are now permitted to sit and try on your boots which should be of the size you told my storeman when he asked. Do not leave here with the wrong size of boots; put on a pair of your issued socks now and remember that your feet will adjust. You have been issued with 2 pairs of ammunition boots and both will require studs to be hammered into the soles.

'Adjust?' What does he mean adjust?' asked Callum Blakie, sitting next to me.

'I think it depends, if you are wearing a forage cap or not.' I replied as I nearly fell off the bench with a nudge from Callum.

'Right everyone, one last item before you leave and that is your greatcoat. I suggest that the easiest way to carry it is to put it on and button it up. Now sign your name at the bottom of the sheet for your issued clothing and equipment and that lets me know that you have all received the correct number of items and that you are happy with their condition.' said the Company Quarter Master Sergeant. 'That being the case,' he continued, 'collect all that you have signed for, pack everything into your kitbag and large pack and move outside where the Trained Soldier will march you back to your accommodation and the other half of the squad can get in to the store.'

When everyone arrived back at the room and all items of kit were lying spread out on their beds, Trained Soldier Woods informed us that there would be no

NAAFI for a few nights and that if anyone wanted drinks or meat pies for later that evening they had better get them at the shop on their way back from tea. 'Tonight you will be introduced to 'Shining Parade',' he said 'and don't forget to lock your locker whenever you are leaving the barrack room.'

'Wow!!' I thought to myself. 'Shining Parade, that should be fun; then I reminded myself not to think too smart or try to be too clever even when I knew that others were harbouring the same thoughts.

'Right,' said the Trained Soldier, 'get all your kit unpacked, folded and placed tidily into your locker. Lay your groundsheet which is also your waterproof cape over your bed and when I have demonstrated how to blanco your webbing which will be in the blanco room, you will lay your wet equipment out on your groundsheets to dry before going for tea. To-night I will be showing you how to press your battledress, lay skins of polish on to your boots ready for bulling up and ensuring that after much spit and polish the toe caps will be gleaming. Your Personal Army Number which you have now been informed of must be stamped on everything that belongs to you; need I say on the inside of all clothing and equipment. Set your number in to the stamp, use it quickly and pass it on to the man in the next bed to you. Memorise your number, I will be testing you. We will work until 10 mins before lights out when you will stop, shower and jump into bed and no I will not be tucking you up. Any questions?'

'No Trained Soldier,' was the immediate, unanimous response.

'Have you memorised your army number yet?' whispered Pete McKinley.

'I think I've written it down and it's under my pillow,' I said. 'I'm frightened of mixing it up with my mother's St Cuthbert's Co-op number.'

'I don't think that will help her dividend,' he said and we both burst out laughing.

The night passed quickly, 'lights out' was sounded and darkness fell on the Guards Depot.

Chapter 5 - Life in the Scots Guards

The following morning, the duty piper played reveille outside the hut and we leapt out of bed knowing that within minutes the Trained Soldier would be in with a bucket of cold water to throw on anyone caught still in bed.

'Stand by your beds.' He shouted, as he entered the room.

Immediately we stopped making up our beds and stood to attention at the bottom of our beds.

'This morning you will wear your denims and plimsolls. Get your beds made up now. Get washed, shaved, dressed and double over to the cookhouse for breakfast. As soon as you get back get the floor swept and bumpered. All ledges are to be dusted; toilets, baths, showers and blanco room scrubbed out and your room is to be spotless and immaculate. I will then brief you on todays programme. 'Do you understand me?'

'Yes Trained Soldier.' We responded as expected.

'Any questions?'

'No Trained Soldier.'

'Good; now get your tired, idle, bodies moving. Guardsman Gee,' he shouted, 'what's your army number?'

'23517903 Trained Soldier,' I replied immediately to my surprise.

'Well done. I bet you're glad I didn't ask you to say it backwards,' he said as he went out the door.

All the lads gave me a big clap and I felt good on my first morning of training.

After breakfast and the morning cleaning had been inspected by the Trained Soldier, we paraded outside in our denims and PT shoes to await the arrival of our Squad Instructor L/Sgt Bath. As he approached Trained Soldier Woods called us to attention and reported that the squad was ready for his inspection.

'Thank-you Trained Soldier. Well I hope you all made a good start last night in sorting out your bed space, tidying your kit and getting to know your equipment as well as each other, and of course had a good night's sleep.

'Yes we did, Sergeant.' we replied.

'Good, we have a busy day ahead of us and I will brief you now although some details may change as the day progresses. Sergeant Rudd who is your Superintendent Sergeant will be along shortly and sometime later this morning Your Company Commander Major Nicholson wishes to meet you. Today will be spent pressing your uniform, blancoing your belt and cleaning the brasses with the NAAFI'S best tins of bluebell. Your boots require having the studs hammered in and skins of polish put on them ready for bulling up until you can see your face in the toe caps. One pair will become your best boots for wearing on parade and during inspections. It appears that Thomson and Drummond are well ahead in sorting out their kit and I have decided to make them Squad Leaders for the present. They will help anyone in the squad who is falling behind in getting their kit up to scratch.'

'There will be a squad photograph taken when I think that you are ready, to send one home to your mothers which no doubt you will, and sometime this week you will visit our Church of Scotland padre or the priest depending on your denomination of choice. Any Episcopalians can see the Church of England Minister whom I understand is quite a nice chap. Everyone will attend the church parade on Sunday morning.'

'As from today, all instructions for the following day will be posted after tea on the Company Notice Board, and do not fail to read them; I repeat do not fail to read them. Ensure that you understand where you have to be and what duties you are required to carry out as laid down by those orders.'

'Stand to attention now,' shouted Sgt Bath as a new Sergeant appeared wearing a red sash across his chest and what we found out later was called a pace stick tucked under his left arm. L/Sgt Bath, walked forward to meet the new Sergeant, placing his left foot on to the ground, prior to bending his right knee and crashing his right foot down to land exactly beside his left boot. 'Squad ready for inspection Sergeant,' he shouted.

'Thank-you Sgt Bath. I would like to speak to the squad; ask them to stand at ease please.'

Sgt. Bath turned to face us. 'This is Sergeant Rudd your Superintendent Sergeant. Listen carefully to what he has to say. Stand at ease, feet astride and hands clasped behind your back.'

'You have chosen to join the best infantry regiment in the world,' said Sgt Rudd 'and when you have completed your training you will be proud to join your battalion as a member of the Regiment of Scots Guards. We have two battalions whilst most regiments have only one. It's very important that you learn your Regimental History and I'm quite sure that you will be testing each other during shining parade.'

'Tomorrow your training will start in earnest with drill, followed by physical training and a visit to your various padres. A list will go up informing you which fatigues you will be carrying out this weekend; you must check the daily Company Orders without fail. Do not rely on someone else to check it for you. In approximately two weeks you will be moving upstairs into the K Company Block when it is vacated. A notice will be going up on the board asking you to put your names down for which sports you would like to partake in and even represent the Company in the Inter-Company sports. Major Nicholson is now on his way to meet you. Stand to attention and make sure if you are spoken to, you reply clearly and tell the Company Commander that you are happy to be here and that you are very proud to have joined the Regiment.'

He turned away and marched towards the on-coming figure of the Company Commander. We watched in awe out of the corner of our eyes as he came to attention by slamming both feet into the ground in front of Major Nicholson, saluted and said, 'good morning sir, the Squad is formed up and ready for your inspection sir.'

'Thankyou Sergeant Rudd.'

Major Nicholson stepped forward in front of the squad. He was a tall man with a large moustache protruding below his glasses which were perched on his nose and somehow his movement and body language didn't match the slick co-ordination of arms and legs that Lance Sergeant Bath and Sergeant Rudd had.

'Good morning gentlemen,' he said, 'I wish to welcome you to K Company and hope that you will knuckle down to the training that lies ahead of you. I will be following your progress through training closely and I do hope that you will live up to all that is expected of you. You are young and fit, and have chosen a tough regiment to join; the very best. You will be proud to wear our cap badge. Isn't that so Sgt Rudd?'

'Yes sir.'

'If you do have any problems' Major Nicholson continued, 'please speak to your Trained Soldier and Squad Sergeants. My door is always open, should you wish to speak to me. Thankyou Sergeant Rudd,' and as he turned away, he saluted and headed back to his office in the K Company Lines.

'Thankyou sir.' said Sgt Rudd returning the Company Commander's salute.

When the Company Commander had left, Sgt Rudd told us to stand at ease. 'I will now hand you back to Sgt Bath but I will be monitoring your training throughout today. Oh! and by the way Major's Nicholson made a slip of the tongue, his door is not open to you; if you have a problem you already know to speak to your Trained Soldier first and then Sgt. Bath although you may ask to speak to Sgt. Bath privately.'

'Right,' said Sgt. Bath, 'after I call you to attention, I will tell you to fall out. You will turn to your right, pause and then get away into the barrack room where I will speak to you shortly. Do you understand?'

'Yes Sergeant,' we replied.

'Fall out. Now get away quickly you idle shower of men.'

Back in the barrack room, we stood at ease by our beds as Sgt Bath began to inform us as to the programme for the rest of the day. 'As you now know there is a shining parade every evening between 1800 and 2030 hours when you will sit on your beds and clean your kit unless you are standing with an iron in your hand pressing your uniform. Webbing is to be blancoed before tea and laid out to dry on your groundsheets which are to be laid across the bottom of your beds. After tea brasses are to be cleaned and boots polished. Trained Soldier Woods will show you how to place bits of cigarette packets between the brasses to stop bluebell going on to the blanco. You will also have a demonstration of how to get the pimples off your boots and spread a skin of polish on to them by using a spoon, water and black polish but you must first make sure that your boots are fully studded. I understand that you have already been shown how to press your kit; just make sure that there are no double creases and definitely no scorch marks. Guardsmen Thomson and Drummond will be around to help anyone needing assistance.'

'Today will be spent getting all your kit and equipment up to scratch. Company Orders will be on the notice board to-night with other relevant information; make sure that you read and digest them. The Sports Officer has already put up a notice asking for names of those who would like to have a trial for the various Company Sports Teams. I have put everyone's name down for the cross country run which I'm sure you would want to take part in. Am I correct in my assumption?'

'Yes Sergeant.' was the loud reply.

'Good.' he said with a broad grin on his face. 'I have told the Trained Soldier that he may allow you to go to the NAAFI tonight for a short while if he thinks that you have been working hard on your kit. Tomorrow we will be straight into drill followed by PT. If you have no questions you may fall out and go and get a cup of tea at the NAFFI now.' We filed out in an orderly but speedy manner in case there was a change of mind.

As I was at the rear of the squad going out the door, I heard Sgt Bath say, 'They seem a good bunch and I feel that they are going to be a good squad, but keep a grip on them and keep me fully updated on any difficulties that may arise. I'll leave them in your hands Trained Soldier; let's get their kit sorted out and up to scratch. I'll be in the Company Office completing documentation should you need me and I'll call in after lunch. Oh! make sure that they do study their Regimental History.'

'Right sergeant, I will see you later.'

The rest of the day was spent sorting out our kit and when we were told to gather round for the demo of laying a skin of polish on our boots, we did so with anticipation. 'First,' said the Trained Soldier, 'we have to get rid of the pimples on the new leather. Spread a thin layer of polish on to the boot. Heat an old iron which I happen to have and press down on the uppers and around the sides of the boot to remove the pimples. Lay a thick layer of polish on to the whole boot using water with the polish and smooth it into the leather with the back of a spoon. Leave it to dry like this one that I did this morning and then it will be ready for bulling up.' He held up the boot for all to see. 'Wet the corner of the duster and start rubbing in small circles. It is hard work and a second and third skin will be required but I want to see the whole of the boots gleaming. Don't forget to clean the iron after use before passing it on.'

'Stand to attention,' called the Trained Soldier as Sgt Bath entered the room.

'I am Glad to see that you are all busy cleaning your kit. Any problems?'

'No sergeant.'

'Right Smith, what colour is the plume in our bearskins?' asked Sgt Bath

'We are the only infantry regiment in the Brigade of Guards that doesn't wear a plume, sergeant. We don't need one to be recognised.'

'A good answer Smith.'

'Mackintosh, what is the grouping of the buttons down the front of our tunics and why?'

'They are in threes sergeant because we are the Third Regiment in seniority of Foot Guards.'

'Well done. Your turn, Macleod.'

'Yes sergeant.'

'What is the emblem on the collar of our tunic and what is our regimental motto portrayed on our cap badge.'

'It's a thistle Sergeant and our motto is Nemo Me Impune Lacessit; Touch Me Not With Impunity.'

'I can see you have been working hard and studying your history; perhaps in the hope that you might be allowed to go to the NAFFI tonight. Well, all is going to rest on my last question to be answered by...' and there was a long pause. 'As there is so much depending on the correct answer, you can choose whom you wish to answer for you. Any whispering and the answer will not count should it be correct.'

Everyone looked at everyone else and nobody volunteered. 'Howard,' someone shouted and a cheer of agreement echoed around the room. I was mortified.

'Right Gee,' said Sergeant Bath. 'It all depends on you.'

'What is the Scots Guards method of brushing the top of the forage cap?'

There was a deathly hush and all eyes were on me. I couldn't think straight. 'Had we been shown?' I asked myself. I remembered seeing out of the corner of my eye, Trained Soldier Woods brushing his hat before we went to breakfast this morning but my mind was on bacon and eggs, toast and a mug of tea. 'Think Howard; think,' I told myself.

'Wet the brush, hold your hat inside with the flat of your left hand,' I paused. I was going to have to make some sort of guess. 'Hold one end of the brush in the centre of the hat, rotate your right wrist to the left, brushing the hat in a circular movement creating a small circle in the centre and gradually brushing larger ones around the outside.' I said demonstrating with my right hand.

There was another hush and all eyes were on Sgt Bath who looked at me with a blank expression. 'What part of your forage cap do you never touch when picking it up?' he asked

'The peak sergeant.' I answered. 'You place your middle finger of your right hand on top, your forefinger and thumb together with the other finger between the middle and pinkie on the rim and you pick it up.'

He smiled. 'Well done young Gee. I'll confirm with the Trained Soldier that you can all go to the NAAFI tonight but only for an hour.'

The room erupted and I was the hero of the hour.

'Right get on with your kit and I'll see you all tomorrow. I'll leave them in your hands Trained Soldier; make sure that they are all in their beds before lights out.'

'I will Sergeant.'

'Good night to you all.' he shouted as he made his way out of the barrack room into a lovely summer's evening.

'Good night Sergeant,' we shouted.

Chapter 6 - Absent Without Leave

The following morning after breakfast when the room had been cleaned and inspected, the squad formed up in three ranks outside the barrack room in a chirpy, happy mood which was to change the minute Sgt Bath stepped forward and told us to stand at ease which was the basic posture of legs apart and hands behind our backs.

'Good morning,' he said, 'hope you all slept well. If you didn't, don't worry you will to-night.' A strange smile appeared on his face and with that, it all started.

'Squad!' he shouted and we all braced our head and shoulders up and forced our hands down behind our backs. 'Squad shun'; our left legs were raised, knees bent and our left foot crashed down beside our right foot into the position of attention with our hands clenched and pressed into our sides. 'Right turn, quick march,' and we were off; 'left, right, left, right, left, right,' at the pace of an Olympic walker ; 'Squad halt.' We came to a sudden halt falling over each other and bumping into the man in front.

'Right! Stand still, sort yourself out and remember to move both feet forward alternately to the time that is being called out by myself. Do not, I repeat do not move both feet at the same time.' screamed Sgt Bath at the top of his voice. 'Stand to attention now; by the right, quick march, left, right, left, right, squad halt.' and once again we fell forwards into the man in front. 'Stand still. What a shower I've got this time.' he shouted. 'I've seen the Girl Guides and Brownies on their Sunday morning parades with more co-ordination. Now sort yourself out and listen to my commands before we are seen by the Drill Sergeants or even worse the Regimental Sergeant Major. Do you hear and understand me?'

'Yes sergeant.' we all replied

'By the right, quick march,' he shouted and we were off again. 'Left, right, left, right,' and when left wheel was called we took off in different directions; forwards, right and left. Sgt Bath threw his stick on to the ground and his arms up in the air as if he had just had a fit. 'Get back into your three ranks now. Stand to attention and face that way.' he roared pointing with his finger in the direction of the main square. 'By the right, quick march, left, right, left, right, left wheel, squad halt. Stand at ease. Sort your dress out and adjust your berets. Squad!, squad shun, by the right, quick march, left, right, left, right; look to your front; do not dare to let your eyes wander.' shouted Sgt Bath as he saluted a passing officer in the Grenadier Guards who returned the salute without even glancing at the dismal performance of a squad of recruits wearing the Scots Guards badge. Sgt Bath hardly altered his stride and continued his words of command which sounded to us like, 'huf, ight, huf, ight' and although we didn't know what he was shouting, we knew to keep going, one leg in front of the other, arms shoulder high and heads held up. We were shouted, bawled and roared at, chased and hounded around for a further 30 minutes until we were all on the verge of dropping to our knees.

'Squad halt,' was the welcomed command. 'It's now 1000 hours, you have 40 minutes to get back to your room, change into your PT shorts and vest; red vest today, grab your PT shoes and towel, have your NAFFI break and be back here, formed up in three ranks when the Trained Soldier will take you to the gymnasium.' That little smile crossed his face again. 'This afternoon I will be teaching you how to salute. Now when I give you the fall out, remember the count and shout out loud; 1, turn to your right, 2, 3, 1, bend the left knee and drive your foot into the ground, 2, 3, pause and get away quickly. Now listen and get it right,' he shouted. 'Fall out,' came the command and we went through the routine of counting at the top of our voices.

'Fall out?' said Donald Gunn, 'I haven't got the strength to fall over.'

'You'll be alright after a cup of tea and a bacon roll.' I said. 'Let's go and get changed quickly and get over to the NAAFI.' There was a pause while everyone checked that they were still standing upright before making a mad rush into the room and fumbling for the keys to our lockers to get changed and collect our kit.

At the gymnasium, we were met by Sgt Park who ushered us into the changing room to swap our boots for our PT shoes before forming up in the gym which was massive compared to memories of my school gymnasium. There were already two other squads from different regiments who were in advanced weeks of training, judging by their prowess in climbing ropes, vaulting over boxes, tumbling on mats and the circuit training going on amidst a cacophony of grunts, groans, painful sounds and sharp instructions being given out.

After height, weight and chest measurements were taken, we were chased around the gym touching walls from end to end and side to side. We did press ups on the floor, squat jumps with our hands behind our heads and a multitude of exercises that I would never have thought of attempting. At the end of the lesson, we had just enough strength to put our boots back on and get outside where Sgt Park was waiting for us with another Scots Guards PT Instructor whom he introduced as Lance Corporal White. Like Sgt Park, he wore a white sleeveless PT vest with blue serge trousers held up by a red belt with a snake clip fastened at the side of his left hip and black glossed PT shoes on his feet. He was slightly smaller than Sgt Park but very muscular with dark curly hair and when he smiled, a row of gleaming teeth appeared to compliment his broad cockney accent. 'I look forward to seeing you on your next lesson when I'll be assisting Sgt Park,' he said. 'Right Trained Soldier, take them away and go steady with them, they're a wee bit shaky on their pins.'

'A wee bit shaky!' I thought to myself, looking around at the squad who had just staggered out of the changing room and were trying to form up and stand still in a straight line.

'When you get back to your room' said Trained Soldier Woods, 'put your PT shoes and towels in your lockers and stand by your beds for a kit inspection by the Company Orderly Officer of the Day.'

Our beds had been laid out before breakfast with great precision as per. the photograph on the notice board showing the layout for the basic inspection display. On the mattress cover at the top of the bed were two pillows with pillow cases left on, the blankets and sheets were folded and were sitting alternately in a box fashion, blanket, sheet, blanket, sheet, blanket as measured by the room bedding measuring stick. In front were our best highly polished gleaming boots, white mug in the middle and knife, fork and spoon laid out from right to left as the inspecting officer would look at the bed. 'I will call you to attention when Second Lieutenant Pemberton-Smyth arrives. Keep looking to your front and only speak if spoken to. Do you understand me?' asked Sgt Bath who appeared in the doorway.

'Yes sergeant.' was the reply from everyone in the room as we stood by our beds waiting on the presence of the officer whom we knew had arrived when we heard a muffled conversation just outside the door.

'Good morning,' the officer said entering the room followed by Sgt Bath and Trained Soldier Woods who must have felt very important holding a millboard in one hand and a biro pen in the other. They walked around glancing at each bed without any comment and left the room.

'Wow,' said Squad leader Bill Thomson. 'Well done boys.' We all looked round and smiled at each other.

Sgt Bath walked in and the atmosphere changed immediately. The Orderly Officer has reported that he has never seen such a pathetic, dismal layout of kit in his whole army career and wishes to inspect again at 2000 hours tonight. With that Trained Soldier Woods walked around the room tipping every mattress up in the air and on to the floor, scattering our kit everywhere.

'Get this lot sorted out,' shouted Sgt Bath; 'then get over to the dining room for your meal and be formed up outside at 1330 hours. Do you understand me?'

'Yes sergeant.' we shouted as he left the room.

'I don't know if I can take much more of this.' said Rod Graham

'Me too.' echoed Bruce Hall.

'Come on lads, don't let the pressure get to you,' said Squad Leader Jim Drummond. 'It's all part of training designed to make us disciplined Guardsmen. We'll get through it together as a team.'

'How do you know all this Jim?' asked Bruce

'I was in the school Combined Cadet Force,' he answered 'and I had a long chat with my old school teacher who was my Company Commander before I joined up. Although like everyone else, I have a lot to learn, I'm determined that I'm going to enjoy my nine years that I've signed up for and come out a more mature person.'

'Sounds good.' I thought to myself. 'He does seem to have the right attitude but nine years does seem a long time.'

'Howard how long have you signed up for?' asked Rod.

'Three years,' I answered 'and then I want to join the Edinburgh City Police.'

'Bruce and I are six each. If we last that long.' he replied.

'It will pass very quickly; you'll see.' said Bill Thomson

We all stared at Bill shaking our heads with some doubt in our minds.

'Really?' queried Bruce.

'Aye,' said Bill, 'I was well warned that the training would be the most difficult time but once we have completed it, we'll join the battalion and start to enjoy life.'

'Can you give us that in writing?' shouted Donald Gunn and we all burst out laughing.

After dinner, it was more squad drill and marching around individually practicing our saluting which Sgt Bath had demonstrated. First, by coming to a halt e.g. in front of an imaginary officer sitting at his desk, secondly whilst on the march i.e. saluting to the left or right and thirdly when not wearing a hat e.g. when going for meals, an eyes left or right was to be given by turning our heads in the relevant direction whilst our arms were pinned into our sides. 'Watch and I'll demonstrate again.' he said which he did and the movements were clarified. 'Now find a space and work in pairs, saluting each other.'

After a 5 minute smoke break for those that had the weed habit, we were off again. 'Left, right, left, right, left wheel, right wheel, squad halt. Squad shun, quick march' and on and on it went until 1600 hours. Right I am finishing you early to let you go and lay out your kit again for the inspection at 2000 hours. It better be immaculate this time. Also make sure that when you read orders tonight you check which sports you have been selected to take part in later this week.'

That evening, the inspection went well and Second Lieutenant Pemberton-Smyth who wore his very smart and impressive Regimental Officer's Mess Kit walked round asking us where we had come from and generally being interested in how we were settling down to a life in the Scots Guards. Sgt Bath was pleased with the outcome of the inspection and let us all go to the NAAFI for an hour.

The following morning, I was one of the first up; just before reveille and something in the room didn't seem right but I couldn't put my finger on it. I collected my washing and shaving kit from my locker and made my way along to the washroom. In the middle of shaving others were joining me and informing me that Rod Graham and Bruce Hall had gone AWOL.

'What's AWOL?' I asked.

'Absent Without Leave.' said Bill Thomson.

'Don't they shoot you for that?' I asked

Well they did during the war. I don't know what they do now but it's a very serious offence.' said Jim Drummond. 'Certainly time in the cells on bread and water and maybe fifty lashes each.'

There was a sharp intake of breath from someone a few wash basins down from me.

'How do we know that they have gone absent?' asked Pete McKinley

'Because they wirnae there this morning,' Malcolm MacRae answered 'and two sets of pyjamas were found in the toilets. It seems that sometime during the night when the rest of us were in the land of nod, they slipped out, probably heading for London to catch a train home to Bonnie Scotland.'

'Och! If I'd known, I'd have gone with them,' said Tom MacGregor giving us a wink as he stripped off his pyjama jacket to slush cold water under his arms and on to his chest before lathering up for a shave. Getting caught washing or shaving without removing top clothing meant extra fatigue duties.

After breakfast we formed up outside the hut where Sgt Rudd addressed us.

'Well, you will have heard about our two wanderers. They will be caught, probably in the region of Kings Cross Station by the Military Police who have been informed of the situation. As you know you arrived at the Depot carrying only a small case or holdall which was handed into the Quartermaster Stores with the clothes that you were wearing. They will remain there until they are re-issued to you and now you know why. They have only their army battledress and forage caps to wear and they will stick out like a pork chop at a Jewish wedding.

Do not even think of following in their footsteps. Do I make myself clear?'

'Yes sergeant.' we all shouted.

It was another day of drill, physical training, more drill, cleaning the toilets and washrooms with other daily fatigues, but during meals and the lead up to the evening shining parade, the talk was about our two roommates who had gone Absent Without Leave.

Chapter 7 - The Square

The following morning, Sgt Bath announced that the Regimental Sergeant Major had requested that we march on to the rear of the main square and watch the full Depot Morning Parade which we would be joining and taking part in, once we had reached the required standard of drill.

'Tomorrow evening you will be moving into the vacated rooms in K Company lines. You will be upstairs, so prepare yourselves for humping all your bedding, uniforms and kit from here to there with no moaning, fuss or bother involved. Do you understand me?'

'Yes Sergeant.' the standard response was shouted out by all.

'The good news is that you will be nearer the Company Offices where the Company Sergeant Major and the Company Commander will see all your movements and will get to know you better but the bad news for you is that if you are lazy and idle it will be brought to my attention and very quickly, I might add. If by any chance they condescend to speak to you, you will reply and call them what?'

'Sir.' we all shouted out, eager to prove that we knew the answer

'This afternoon is sports afternoon and I see by this list in my hand that you all want to take part instead of doing kitchen fatigues. Gee, I see that you wish to have a trial for a number of sports. Have you played them all before?'

'Yes sergeant.'

'Who did you play football for?'

'United Schools and North Merchiston Boys Club in Edinburgh sergeant.'

'Athletics?' he asked

'Represented the school at athletics, rugby and basketball, sergeant; oh, and cross country running with Braidburn Athletic Club.'

'What else?' he asked.

'Swam for the scouts and played water polo for Warrender Swimming Club in Edinburgh sergeant.'

'You have boxing down here,' he said.

'Leith Victoria.' I replied. 'That's Edinburgh too sergeant.'

'I thought as much,' he said.

'Were you good at any of them?'

'Aye not too bad sergeant.' which I thought was a diplomatic reply.

'We'll soon see.' he said. 'Make sure all of you read the details at dinner time and report to the correct venue at the right time. Don't worry if you are down for more than one trial, the captain of the teams will come and find you and sort out another time later in the week.'

'Now you lot, sort out your dress. Tuck your denim bottoms into your gaiters and adjust your belt and beret; stand up shoulders back and remember when we march on to the square, we are Scots Guards and every step is to be taken with pride. Do not let me down. Do you all understand?'

'Yes sergeant.'

'Good,' he said as he rolled his eyes upwards as if praying for help.

There was a slight chill to the morning and a light breeze was rippling the Depot Flag high up on its pole as we marched on to the rear of the square facing the long avenue stretching from the guardroom down into the heart of the Depot. I couldn't help remembering the day that I arrived at the Depot and had tried to keep up with the Runner as he sped down the avenue. Out of the corner of our eyes we could see the new squads from the other regiments marching on to the left and right of ourselves but resisted the temptation to wave to the lads that we recognised from the Waiting Room. Under their squad instructor's commands, the senior squads taking part in the parade were now marched on to the square and formed up in regimental seniority in front of us. The Regimental Sergeant Major and Drill Sergeant were marching together up and down in step at the front of the parade carrying their pace sticks as if they were an extension of their right arms whilst the junior officers on parade were pacing up and down across the front of the parade ground. The instructors were shouting out orders in a range of dialects to their individual squads ensuring that each rank, front and rear were standing in straight lines. Finally the whole parade was called to attention by Regimental Sergeant Major Rodgers Scots Guards who now took command of the parade.

We had been informed that Regimental Sergeant Major Rodgers came from Glasgow but under threat of a firing squad, we were never to call him by his nickname of Jolly Rodger as in the pirate flag nor ever to refer to him as the RSM; always we were to call him sir. From where we were standing, he looked about eight feet tall with a ram rod straight back. His boots were gleaming and a red sash was worn on his right shoulder, across his chest from right to left and a row of medals were worn above his left breast pocket of his uniform. Around his waist was a white belt with attachments which held his sword on his left hip and on both arms of his jacket just above the elbow was a large badge denoting his rank. We had been informed that only in the Brigade of Guards do Warrant Officers with the rank of Warrant Officer 1 (RSM) wear the large badge of rank whilst all others in the British Army wear a smaller badge lower down above their wrists. He had a small moustache below his nose where the peak of his forage cap carrying three gold bands appeared to be resting. His forage cap carried the red and white dicing and cap badge of the Scots Guards which made us all feel very proud.

Having marched to the centre of the parade, he started to shout to various squad sergeants to dress the

49

rear rank of the Grenadiers forward and the front rank of the Welsh Guards slightly to the left and when he shouted out to one of the squad sergeants 'Remove that piece of fluff from the right shoulder of the third man from the left in the centre rank now.' we were dumbfounded.

The Sergeants In Waiting from each company were called forward with their Company Nominal Roll Books carried in their left hands to report their morning parade attendance figures whilst carrying out a range of very fast drill movements. When the Orderly Officer of the Day came on parade, he was met by the Regimental Sergeant Major who transferred his pace stick from his right hand to under his left arm and saluted. 'Good morning sir.' he said before informing him of the numbers on parade and handing over control of the parade to him. He returned the salute and asked the Regimental Sergeant Major to stand the parade at ease. He in turn asked the junior officers to inspect their regimental squads; they saluted and headed off across the parade to do so accompanied by their Company Sergeant Majors and Company Sergeants in Waiting. He and the Drill Sergeant made their way to a squad of Grenadiers.

When the Regimental Sergeant Major looked in our direction and started marching towards our squad at the rear of the parade, I think we all shut our eyes and thought 'Oh, no.'

'Sergeant Bath,' he shouted, 'I would like to say a few words to your squad.'

'Certainly sir.' said Sergeant Bath standing to attention and stepping to one side.

'It's good to see you on parade this morning.' said the Regimental Sergeant Major. 'I have been watching you and I am very glad to see you have stood to attention without fidgeting. It will not be long before you are taking part in the parade and I would assure you all that you have chosen to join the very best regiment in the army and hope that you will be a credit to your instructor. You lad,' he said, pointing his pace stick at me, 'what's your name?'

'Recruit Gee sir.' I answered feeling my knees beginning to wobble.

'What year was your regiment raised?'

'1642 sir.'

'Well done young man.' he said. 'I look forward to seeing you all on my parade again. Thank you Sergeant Bath.' He turned sharply and marched off across the parade ground, shouting various comments and instructions at the squad non-commissioned officers on parade

It was just at that moment when Sergeant Bath was saying 'well done' that he realised that the whole squad was looking past him at the long avenue where two figures wearing battledress but no belts nor hats were being marched one behind the other from the guardroom past the parade ground with a sergeant shouting out, 'left, right, left, right, left, right' as quick as his mouth would open and shut. They were struggling to keep their legs moving in time with the instructions being called out.

It was Rod and Bruce; now prisoners under escort and they appeared to be heading from the guardroom towards the Commandant's Office.

Chapter 8 - A New World

As we were all involved with sports that afternoon we were more than happy to settle down to shining parade after tea. As we sat on our beds cleaning our kit, the silence was suddenly broken when the doors burst open and the sombre faces of Rod and Bruce entered, carrying blankets, sheets and pillows. They headed over to their bed spaces where their mattresses had been folded over awaiting use. The excitement of their return was quickly dampened down by the entrance of Trained Soldier Woods who ordered everyone to be quiet and get on with cleaning our kit. 'You two,' he shouted, 'put your bedding down and get over to the stores to collect your kit. Now!!'

'Yes Trained Soldier.' they replied as they pulled their mattresses over, dropped their bedding on to them and went back out the door almost falling over each other.

We sat looking at each other in a daze until the voice of the Trained Soldier filled the room. 'Get on with your cleaning now and don't let me hear another word from any of you. Do not speak or confer with those two at all when they return or you will be filling their vacant cells in the guardroom. Do you understand?'

'Yes Trained Soldier.'

Later that night whilst someone kept a lookout for the Trained Soldier, Bruce and Rod related their tale of woe. After lights out, they had pretended to go to the toilet, where they changed from pyjamas into uniform and managed to slip out a small back gate used by families from the married quarters going to and fro to the NAFFI shop. They caught a taxi to the railway station at Caterham and a late night train to London, hoping to catch the first train going north in the morning to Scotland. They were looking at the huge timetable board in Kings Cross Station when two military policemen asked if they could see their Identity Cards.

They tried explaining that they were recruits and hadn't yet been issued with them but they had been allowed home on compassionate leave to see Rod's sister who had just had a baby. 'I don't understand why the two corporals burst out laughing and asked to see our leave passes.' said Bruce. After that we were handcuffed and taken by land rover to Military Police cells in central London where we spent a few hours before being delivered back to the guardroom here at the Guards Depot early this morning.

'Welcome back.' said Murdoch MacLeod.

'Aye.' we all agreed.

It was 1930 hours when the Trained Soldier came back into the room. 'Make sure that you read orders if you haven't already done so.' he said. 'The Depot will be in shirt sleeve order tomorrow and as you know your sleeves are to be rolled up to the regulation height above the elbow and pressed accordingly. Battledress trousers will be worn with blancoed belt and gators. Needless to say you are to be immaculately turned out with boots gleaming, not just your toe caps and heels. As you know after tea tomorrow, you will be moving into your new accommodation; try to make a start on packing the kit that you are not wearing or using tomorrow. It's going to be a hard day; be prepared for it. Right!' he said, 'you can go to the NAAFI for an hour. Not you two.' he said pointing at Rod and Bruce. 'You can get on with getting your kit up to scratch for the morning or you will be back in the cells.'.

We all returned early from the NAAFI that night to finish off cleaning our kit and ensure that we were ready for the following morning. We had brought back extra steak pies, biscuits and coffee in paper cups to share with the two lads which they placed under their beds out of sight. Bruce gave us a big grin and Rod gave the thumbs up sign. I remember the words teamwork and friendship coming into my mind.

The following morning we were formed up and ready waiting for Sergeant Bath; back to a full squad again except for Walter Johnston who had decided to go on sick parade with a boil somewhere on his rear end. He was receiving little sympathy from the squad and when Malcolm MacRae said that they still used leeches in the Guards to suck out the puss and they would be crawling all over his private parts, Walter turned pale and almost passed out. It was a good laugh to start off the day although a cold shiver ran up my bare arms and I hoped that the warmth of the morning sun was on its way. Obviously we were going to have to get used to shirt sleeve order.

We had drill, more drill and a double period of physical training where we were introduced to the three mile run which nearly killed the whole squad and we were lucky to be able to reach the NAAFI for our morning break. When we formed up again, we were now told that the big accommodation move had now been brought forward to immediately after our early lunch which had been arranged with the Colour Sergeant in the cookhouse.

'I understand from the sports captains that we have some talented sportsmen in our squad and that we will be well represented in the Depot Teams,' said Sergeant Bath. 'Make sure that you do read Company Orders to see when you have been chosen to play. Well done to you all and a special mention to MacAlistair, Smith, Blakie, McKinlay and Gee to be chosen for athletics, swimming, water polo and basketball. The trials for football, rugby and cross country will be a little later in the season but trials for the Inter Company Boxing Championships are to be held soon followed by training. We are now going back to the room where the Trained Soldier will show you how to make up your weekly laundry submission.'

'You are allowed eight items of clothing each week,' said the Trained Soldier, 'which are to be ticked off on your issued laundry label. Your selected items are to be rolled into your towel, tied with string and your label tied to the string. Need I say that you must put your name and number on the label? Yes I think I must say.' he said looking around the room. 'Remember it will be a week before they come back. Do not send items that will be needed during that week. If I may suggest pyjamas 1pr, vest and under pants 1 of each, shirt 1, denim jacket and trousers 1set and make sure the jacket buttons are unhooked and fitted on to your clean jacket; socks 1pr, one item of choice and a towel. The rest you can wash with your tiny hands but rubber gloves are not to be worn unless you are a qualified midwife. Make up your bundle now and leave it outside the room front door for the Quartermaster's staff to pick up in readiness for collection by the laundry company. As soon as you have finished, get away for dinner. Do you understand me?'

'Yes Trained Soldier.'

'Any questions?'

'No Trained Soldier.' we shouted as he left the room.

'What did he say again?' asked Tom Macgregor

'Only one blanket and two sheets at a time.' replied Hamish MacPherson

'Ignore him Tom.' I said, 'Sheets and pillow slips are exchanged every Wednesday morning as you know.'

'Once a month.' said Ewan Stuart and we all burst out laughing.

Throughout the afternoon we were like the Israelites moving into the Promised Land. With arms full of kit, equipment and bedding, we were up and down the stairs but felt good about moving into K Company proper along with the other senior Scots Guards Squads in training. Being upstairs looking down over the veranda at bodies scurrying to and fro, created a feeling of being part of a whole new world. Nobody ever strolled casually along in the Depot. The washrooms, toilets and blanco room were to our left along the veranda and to reach them, we had to pass a very formidable looking door carrying a sign with the word Armoury in large letters.

The new room had ten beds down each side with a wooden locker in between each bed and a row of large windows on one side which could be left open to let the fresh Surrey air circulate throughout the day and night. With seventeen of us all sharing the one room, summer nights could be quite stifling.

'Graham, you and Hall, take the two beds nearest the doorway, one at either side where I can keep my eyes on you both. My bunk is in the corridor just outside the room and you will keep the room door open at all times until I say otherwise. Is that clear?'

'Yes Trained Soldier.'

'Now get your beds made down, lockers dusted, kit hung up, bed spaces cleaned, floor swept and polish laid down ready for bumpering up tomorrow morning. The windows and sills inside are to be cleaned. The veranda outside is our responsibility for cleaning as are all the toilets, showers, baths, wash basins and of course the blanco room. You are now free until tomorrow morning to get our accommodation up to scratch. Squad Leaders Drummond and Thomson, check what cleaning materials are left in the large cleaning locker. Then go over to the Q.M. stores and draw up whatever is required. If brooms, mops, shovels, bumper handles are broken and required to be exchanged, take the old ones with you or you will not get new ones issued. You will have to sign for the new equipment. Any questions?'

'No Trained Soldier.'

'Oh one further thing you will have noticed that you pass the armoury as you go to the ablutions. Do not think about raiding it and seeking revenge on all who have upset you during your stay at the Depot. Am I clear?'

'Yes Trained Soldier.'

'Do you think he has a sense of humour?' someone asked as he left the room.

'No!' we all shouted.

'I heard that.' came a voice from the corridor.

Chapter 9 - Our Squad

We settled down into our new accommodation and began to feel and believe that we were beginning to be worthy of being called Scots Guardsmen. Loyalty to our squad grew and as a team we began to believe that we could overcome any difficulties that arose throughout our training at the Depot.

We had drill, physical training, swimming and appropriate physical tests to ensure that we were progressing towards worthy trained soldiers, capable of carrying out the military roles that was expected of the Regiment. Fatigues, mainly at weekends in the cookhouse, consisted of peeling spuds, scrubbing dixies, washing dishes, wiping down tables, emptying slops, filling urns of tea which we all believed was full of bromide to kill our sexual urges, mopping floors and a hundred and one other jobs that the cook Sergeant had on his daily list of chores. All the cooks and dining staff were themselves members of the regiments within the Brigade of Guards. In the sergeant's mess, the fatigues were mainly polishing and bumpering the floors of the main entrance, hallway and snooker room. Chairs and tables were moved around to cater for their different functions held in the lounge, and there was no shortage of allocated tasks in the kitchen not to mention sweeping and shovelling up anything around the grounds that moved and was an intruder to cleanliness or tidiness.

From reveille in the morning to lights out at night, we just never stopped and barely had time to enjoy the wonderful Surrey sunshine and warm weather. After shining parade each evening, we looked forward to being allowed to attend the NAAFI at night where we had a few pints of beer and a good laugh. We listened to the lads in the senior squads and joined in a bit of banter with the recruits from the other regiments, taking up challenges in darts and dominoes. Discipline was strict and failing to carry out instructions efficiently and immediately when given by instructors would result in the whole squad being punished which encouraged teamwork and pride in all the activities undertaken.

We were told one night at the NAAFI about a squad of Grenadiers who had failed a major inspection because one member of their squad hadn't spent time cleaning his kit properly and they had all been punished with extra drilling and fatigues on their free week-end. The guilty party was subjected in the middle of the night by his squad, to a regimental bath in cold water and scrubbed with a bass broom which was officially not allowed and never spoken of except within the confines of squads in training, and no-one ever complained.

Some of the lads had joined the army from an unhappy home life; some from having been in minor trouble and had been given the choice of a custodial sentence or signing on the dotted line to serve Her Majesty. Some had never been away from home and had joined up for adventure and some were married and had babies or young children at home, but all at one time or another felt pangs of home sickness. Often during the night, sobbing could be heard especially after someone had returned from a long phone call home or a very private letter had arrived which visually affected the receiver. I had only ever been away from home for two weeks at a time on a number of consecutive years when camping with the scouts. I think in retrospect that helped me cope with missing home comforts but I was very much missing Carmine who had pressed into my hand a Saint Christopher's Medal as I left Edinburgh and boarded the London train. 'It will keep you safe.' she said, and I found solace and strength from it as I carried it around my neck day and night. The Regimental Padres were always on hand to have a chat with anyone having a 'breakdown' moment.

The nights, days and weeks rolled by and we gradually started to accept discipline, the ability to carry out orders and complete given tasks at double quick time without questioning the logic of the commands given.

One day we were asked by Sgt Bath if the squad would be willing to assist in a voluntary capacity; the local old age pensioners group who were having a celebration of one of their members who had received an honour from her Majesty for services to the Territorial Army. We would be helping to lay out the tables and chairs in the hall, serve the meals and one of our most important tasks would be to assist the aged who had difficulties with their walking and help those as required with their wheel chairs. The response was a unanimous yes, especially when we were told that we would receive a meal and a beer after tidying up at the end of the night and that the driver of the Depot Coach would take us to the hall and return us to the Depot at the end of the evening.

Over seventy people attended, mostly old soldiers wearing rows of medals, with their wives some whom were also wearing medals, and did they all let their hair down. They were met at the door and given a warm welcome by the organisers. The meal was superb and having been given a half hours training, the service at the tables was second to none, or we thought so anyway. Although mention was made of the distinguished guests, the speeches were kept to a minimum and after the meal the port was passed to the left around the table and the toast to The Health of Her Majesty The Queen was taken. Whilst coffee and tea was being served a comfort break was announced although it had been understood that owing to the senior ages of those attending, leaving the tables for the toilets was permissible at any time.

'You may now smoke,' announced the MC for the evening and as cigarettes, pipes and the occasional cigar was lit, conversations burst out around the hall.

After most had returned to their seats and made themselves comfortable, the band started playing a variety of well-known old favourites and when the 'Boys of the Old Brigade' was struck up, the old soldiers could hardly sit still. Two with walking sticks on their shoulders assimilating rifles started marching up and down between the tables albeit slowly, others joined in behind them. All sang heartily and when an encore was called for, the cheers resounded throughout the hall; the atmosphere was fantastic and many of the old folks had a tear in their eye as personal memories were brought back to them. Throughout the evening we enjoyed speaking to the guests and answering their questions about how we were enjoying army life and especially in the Guards.

At the end of the night, a vote of thanks was given to all who had organised and made the evening such a success. We in the Scots Guards were given a special mention which made us all feel very proud. Thank goodness other helpers had agreed to do all the washing up.

We awoke the following day at reveille to the strains of the bagpipes played by the duty piper and another day had begun. We were becoming quite good at drill and after the first ten minutes each day of being rifted around, Sgt Bath would settle us down to a slower pace where we could hold our heads up , shoulders back and feel proud as we marched through the K Company Lines; progressing to around the Depot and on to the square. One day, a treat was in store when we were told that we were going to learn to slow march and after a few lessons, we even had a trainee piper from the Piping School which was located nearby to assist us by playing the 'Garb of Old Gaul,' the Regimental Slow March. Sometimes ,depending on the weather, we were marched back and forwards in the huge drill sheds often having to share with squads from other regiments but nobody seemed to mind the competitive comments between the instructors and each squad tried hard to show the others how drill should be done. On wet days, waterproof capes which doubled up as groundsheets were worn when moving around the Depot keeping us dry and anything else we carried underneath such as PT kit tucked under our left arm, allowing our right arm still to swing forwards and backwards to the time being called out by Sgt Bath; nothing stopped the training programme.

One night the Company Memoranda on the notice board informed us that Major Nicholson, the Company Commander, would be carrying out a kit inspection the following morning and we were to stand by our beds at 0900hrs. All items of kit were to be laid out on the bed as per the photograph pinned up on the notice board.

This was to be a full kit inspection which included folded blankets and sheets laid out and measured in box fashion as normal. Water bottle with cork left out, gaiters and folded PT vests red and white were to be placed on the top blanket with a folded and pressed shirt sitting in front of the bottom blanket. Best boots, woollen socks, mess tins, PT shoes with soles upwards and polished black, were all to be laid out; one of each at either side of a white towel stretched out on the centre of the bed. A tin of blanco and black boot polish with an assortment of brushes were placed in a line at the bottom of the bed. On the towel were 1 pair of boot laces, shaving brush, shaving soap and razor, comb, toilet soap, knife fork and spoon, housewife, 6 shirt buttons and 2 balls of wool darning. On top of the housewife (pouch container for all sewing items) which was placed in the middle of the towel, a thimble sat on a reel of thread and in the very centre was a long darning needle with two smaller sewing needles laid out in the shape of a K representing K Company. Sgt Bath told the Trained Soldier to open the windows and allow some air to circulate around the room.

We could hear the footsteps on the stairs and as we stood in trepidation by our beds looking to our fronts, Sgt Bath called us to attention and saluted the Company Commander as he entered the room.

'Good morning sir, the squad is ready for your inspection sir.'

Good morning and thank-you Sgt Bath.' he replied as he returned the salute. 'I'd be grateful if you would accompany me and make a note of any pertinent comments.'

'Yes sir; of course sir,' was the speedy reply.

As the Company Commander approached, we individually had to call out our army number, rank which was Recruit and surname followed by a loud 'sir,' so that he knew to whom he was addressing. He walked around each bed space looking at the kit and equipment, running his hand along the tops of the lockers, lifting up and inspecting our gleaming boots, looking at the inside and the reverse side of mess tins and squinting at various other items of kit. He made some comments, spoke to a few individuals and asked a few questions as he passed by each bed.

'Thank you gentlemen.' he said. 'I'm delighted that you are all enjoying your training and are fast becoming trained soldiers who can wear the Scots Guards badge with pride although there is a long way to go yet. Well done indeed.' He saluted and left the room followed by Sgt Bath and Trained Soldier Woods. Still standing to attention, we looked around and smiled at each other.

After a couple of minutes Sgt Bath, our Trained Soldier and another from the senior squad on the ground floor returned to the room. 'Right!' he said 'What a shambles that was. Kit was not laid out as per the demonstration photograph, boots were not polished to standard, mess tins were dirty, needles were not shining, thread was not the right colour, the correct number of buttons were not on display; in fact there were so many things showing in bad order that I ran out of paper on my mill board. There will be another full inspection tomorrow morning at 0900hrs and there had better be a vast improvement. Do I make myself clear?'

'Yes Sergeant.' was the loud response.

'You will remain standing to attention by your beds until you are dismissed. Trained Soldier Woods assisted by Trained Soldier Martin will take the appropriate action. Do you understand?'

'Yes sergeant.'

As Sgt Bath left the room, the two Trained Soldiers started at the door, lifted up every second mattress full of kit and threw them out of the open windows. We continued to look to our fronts, gritted our teeth, wanted to cry but couldn't force the tears out through the anger and dismay. Having completed their work which we were sure they enjoyed, they stomped out and before closing the door, Trained Soldier Woods looked over his shoulder and shouted, 'You've got fifteen minutes to get downstairs, retrieve all your kit and be formed up outside in three ranks ready for swimming.'

Bill Thomson and Jim Drummond stepped into the centre of the room together. Jim held up his hand and spoke. 'We will now muck in and help each other to collect our kit and bring it back upstairs, tidy it away until tonight when we will clean it again and have it ready for inspection tomorrow morning.'

'No grumping, no groaning,' said Bill. 'Do I make myself clear? Do you understand?' he said, imitating Sgt Bath.

We looked at him and burst out laughing.

The inspection went well the following morning and that afternoon when we had our official squad photograph taken, our spirits were high and we were beginning to realise that discipline and a sense of humour were now part of our lives.

Chapter 10 - Fitness and Discipline

I was now playing and enjoying football, basketball, water polo and was selected to swim in the inter-company championships which we won. K Company was second in the athletics although I managed to come second in the individual three miles and was a member of the 4x400 yards winning relay team. I won the individual javelin and high jump and little did I realise that I had placed my foot on the first rung of the ladder towards my future in the army. Rugby and cross country running would start later on in the year. Hopefully we would have completed our military training by that time, had our Passing Out Inspection and moved from The Guards Depot to The Guards Training Battalion at Pirbright in Surrey to complete the six weeks of battle training before becoming fully fledged Scots Guardsmen. We all agreed that the most important happening would be the seven days leave between the moves from Caterham to Pirbright when we would be allowed to travel home in uniform.

Trials were held to represent the company at boxing and I was selected for the team which meant early morning runs and training in the evenings after shining parade but we were awarded extra rations to build up our stamina and that was a welcomed perk. The coaches were our PT Instructors who were determined that we would be fit for the championships and fit we were. Training consisted of skipping, shadow boxing, using punch pads, heavy punch bags, ducking and weaving, and of course, sparring. The Inter Company Boxing was very competitive and each regiment desperately wanted to win and tried hard to ensure that their representatives competing at each weight were kept a secret. Training was kept within their own company lines although quite often teams would bump into each other on early morning runs when all sorts of gestures were interchanged. The Irish Guards were the favourites going by previous years but we had heard that this year, they were worried by the rumours circulating around the NAAFI, mainly spread by ourselves about the strength of the Jocks.

The weights ranged from lightweight to heavyweight and each of the five infantry regiments had a representative at each weight. The first three drawn out of the hat at each weight received a bye leading into the semi-finals and the finals. I was selected at Light Middle Weight weighing-in on the scales at 11 stone two pounds, bang on the maximum limit. The competition was held over two afternoons with the final on the third evening and I had managed to win through to the final where the gymnasium was packed and the atmosphere was electric. Although the Welsh and Coldstreams were slightly behind on points, the Grenadiers, Irish and ourselves were neck and neck. I had been told that the lad that I was boxing had won the County Armagh Championships and had been in the running for the Northern Ireland Team before joining the army, and although I was very nervous I knew that I would try my best. We were introduced to the spectators by the Regimental Sergeant Major who was the Master of Ceremonies. I could see that my opponent and I were both about the same height with a similar arm reach but there was a film of vaseline covering a scar above his right eye where stitches had at one time been inserted, portraying some experience in his boxing prowess and the tricks of his coaching team.

When the cheering died down, the referee stepped forward and called us both to the centre of the ring. He looked closely at my opponent, retrieved a towel from his corner, wiped the vaseline off and returned the towel to his second. 'You know that is not allowed.' he said as he turned back to address us. 'Stop boxing and stand back if told to do so. If I speak to one of you, or stop the bout for any reason, the other must go to a neutral corner. In the event of one or both of you being knocked down on to the canvas, you must listen to my count, stand up, wipe your gloves on your shorts and commence boxing on the command box. Do you understand? Shake hands now; return to your corners and commence boxing when the bell rings. Let's have a good clean spirited contest.'

Sgt Park slipped my gum shield into my mouth and climbed out of the ring as the bell rang for the first round. Recruit O'Sullivan came out of his corner full of confidence, met me in the centre of the ring and immediately scored a point with a straight left to the chin and another on to my nose. He followed up with a left hook to the side of my head which sent me reeling against the ropes and I had to adapt a defensive stance by covering up, trying to counter attack by throwing some straight rights and moving away out of trouble. The bell went and I was glad to return to my red corner and sit on the stool whilst wondering what I had got myself into. Sgt Park removed my gum shield, dropped it into a beaker of water, and sponged me down with his right hand whilst easing out with his left the waist band of my shorts to help control my breathing. After a few wafts of the towel, he said something about keeping my guard up and continuing to move out of trouble. He assisted me off the stool and slipped my gum shield back into my mouth before ducking under the ropes as Cpl White pulled the stool away.

The bell announced the second round and being a southpaw and leading with my right hand, I managed to score with a feint jab and a straight right to his chin. He reeled backwards and I followed through with a straight left which connected to his forehead. My confidence grew a little and throughout the round, I managed to hold my own although he caught me twice to the body just as the bell went. I was glad to return to my corner again, feel the wet sponge on my brow and listen to my coach. As I sat on my stool, I glanced across at my opponent who wasn't even sitting down in his corner; either he was feeling extremely fit or he was too frightened to sit on his stool in case he couldn't get up; I hoped it was the latter. 'You're down on points. You've got three minutes to go; you need a stoppage or a knockout.' said Sgt Park as he helped me off the stool again and nudged me back into the ring to coincide with the bell ringing for the third and last round. We circled around each other throwing a few feints, straight punches, jabs, parrying and blocking with gloves and elbows when suddenly we found ourselves in one of the corners holding on and pulling each other in close.

'Break,' called the referee and as we both stood back, I realised that he was breathing heavily, dropping his arms and tiring rapidly. This was my chance to step forward, feint with a right to the body, bring two short quick punches up to his face and follow through with a straight left to his chin. He was too slow in covering up with his gloves and swerved slightly to his left and backwards; I followed through with a right uppercut under his chin and a left hook to his jaw. His knees buckled and he crashed to the floor and was still on one knee when the referee counted to ten. Our jubilant supporters in the hall were shouting and cheering and the competition was now neck and neck between the Jocks and the Micks. It all depended on the last bout of the evening, the Welterweight and what a match, it turned out to be. We won it on a point's decision, collected the shield and retired to the NAAFI for jubilant celebrations.

At reveille next morning we were up, washed, shaved, had breakfast and were on the square for drill but there was one major difference in our drill lesson; we had now been issued with rifles. Prior to drill each day we had now to draw up and sign individually from the armoury a self-loading rifle (SLR) and had to learn how to hold it, carry it and treat it with the utmost respect. As with all weapons when in training never to point them at anyone. Under the observant eye of the armourer, we held the weapon pointing upwards and had to ensure by pulling back the cocking handle twice, releasing it and pulling the trigger that there were no rounds in the chamber or up the barrel. The rifle was then held up at the port position for inspection and confirmation by the armourer that the chamber was empty of all rounds. All weapons had of course been checked before being taken into the armoury but there was no room for complaisance and all weapons had to be cleared before they were taken from the area.

Later on in our training at Pirbright, after firing on the ranges, we would have to check all pockets and equipment before leaving the range and individually make the declaration of:

'I have no live rounds or ammunition in my possession sir.' and a court martial could be the result of making a mistake.

We had to learn how to load rounds into the magazine, unload the weapon, strip, clean, oil and put all the parts together again in working order with blindfolded speed competitions assimilating usage in conditions of conflict. In our weapon training pouches, we always carried a small piece of felt measuring 4x2 inches with a small bottle of oil from which a little was dropped on to the felt before attaching it to one end of a long piece of thin rope known as a pull through. A small lead weight on the other end was dropped through the barrel and pulled through to clean it. Cleanliness was imperative towards ensuring that the working parts were in perfect working order and that the weapon was always ready for immediate action and didn't jam through neglect when required to be used.

Weapons were always checked by the armourer when handed in and if the barrel had a speck of dirt in it, restriction of privileges were fast and furious. 'You could plant tatties in there.' was a commonly used term by the armourer and punishment was often helping him to carry out cleaning chores in the evenings within the armoury when agreed by the Trained Soldier.

Once we had mastered carrying the rifle by the hand grip pressed firmly into our sides as at the drill position, we were each issued with a bayonet and were taught how to fix and unfix it on parade. Marching with a bayonet fixed to a rifle instead of just carrying it on the hip in its frog required a lot more care and attention when carrying out drill movements within the squad. One day we were formed up outside the barrack room waiting on Sgt Bath to arrive and march us on to the square for the morning parade. Trained Soldier Woods was doing his usual quick inspection of the squad and had almost reached the end of the front rank when he let out a yell.

'What's that mark on your belt?' he screamed out and as he bent forwards and closer to inspect it, Donald Gunn leaned forward to see what he was talking about and his bayonet knocked the Trained Soldier's forage cap off his head and caused him to turn as pale as a bed sheet. He stood with his mouth wide open staring at Donald, unable to speak.

'Sorry.' said Donald and stepped forward to retrieve his cap.

'Get f.......... back in line. I'll get my own f.......... hat.' shouted the Trained Soldier who had now gone scarlet with sheer fright and embarrassment.

The rest of us in the squad remained standing to attention and in spite of what could have been a serious situation, we burst out laughing.

'You missed him Donald.' someone whispered from the rear rank.

Trained Soldier Woods went berserk bawling and shouting at Donald and the squad for laughing but by the time Sgt Bath arrived, we were standing to attention looking to our front and not another word was spoken about the incident except in the room after lights out when a good laugh was at its best.

Physical training was now more strenuous and tested us to the limit. Completion of the assault course wearing full battle order involved climbing and traversing high ropes, six and twelve foot walls where success depended on teamwork. High aerial walks from tree to tree, across rope bridges, crawling through narrow pipes and tunnels full of water which when wearing helmets and packs on our backs always carried the fear of getting wedged or sinking below the water itself, not to mention claustrophobia.

We stood on a high bank at the edge of the huge water ditch which we had to swing across on a rope and jump off on to the wet muddy landing area at the far side, providing the rope had enough momentum to swing the length of the ditch. Malcolm MacRae, swung, didn't reach the far bank and was on his way back hanging on to the rope when Tony Mackintosh, awaiting his turn, all keyed up to go, jumped on to the rope which now swung back and because of the extra weight stopped near the middle of the ditch. Both let out a yell as they slid down the rope and plunged into the beckoning black foul smelling, slimy water. The air was blue with the curses and incomprehensible language although there was no doubt as to what the instructors were insinuating. The situation was made worse by the laughter from a nearby Welsh Guards squad sharing the assault course and who were practising lifting and carrying each other over their shoulders assimilating wounded men being carried to safety from the field of battle. One lad slipped and fell on to his knees, dropping his wounded comrade and received the verbal wrath of his instructor and although we felt sorry for him, vengeance was sweet.

Our two lads crawled out of the water and up the bank like prehistoric creatures emerging from the murky deep, covered in slime. We rushed to help them on to their feet but they were bawled at and told immediately to get back on to the rope; one at a time of course and complete their task. There was always the possibility of falling twisting a knee or an ankle and injuring oneself resulting in being back-squaded and not being able to attend the Passing Out Inspection with their squad; being back-squaded and having to repeat some weeks of training was a real fear for all recruits.

Close combat and self-defence were a popular part of training but physical fitness tests of stamina when cold and wet combined with agility, balancing, strength exercises, climbing and running were not enjoyable. Three and five mile runs were now regular and required all the will power that one could muster. We all knew about and dreaded, the ten mile bash in full battle order.

Failures caused the whole squad to have a re-run and it was therefore in everyone's interest for the whole squad to pass first time; grit, determination and teamwork was imperative to success. A piper always accompanied the ten mile bash to play when the pace was flagging and spirits required lifting.

There was great joy and jubilation by all when we returned one Saturday afternoon with a 100% passes from the run. After cleaning our weapons and handing them into the armoury, showering, attending to blisters, cuts and bruises, we cleaned all our kit and webbing, washed our clothes and headed to the NAFFI for celebrations, a good laugh and a bit of boasting to all within as to how easy it had been. Our spirits were soaring high.

I had been selected to play football for the Company team at right half against a Coldstream team one sunny warm Saturday afternoon. I made my way over to the football pitches wearing the number 4 jersey and carrying my boots. I was feeling good and enjoying life until skirting the main square when I heard the Drill Sergeant's voice even before I saw the six lads on Extra Drills. They were wearing full denims with their great coats on top and a large pack full of kit on their backs. Their legs inside their trousers which were tucked into their gaiters were going backwards and forwards like the pendulum of a clock that had gone wild. Their forage caps were wobbling about on their heads and I could see by the coloured banding on their hats that they were from the Grenadiers and Irish regiments. What they had been up to I had no idea but it could have ranged from being idle or having polished boots below standard on parade to having unclean belt brasses or dust on their locker tops during an inspection. I felt sorry for them being rifted around as I glanced up at the sun and visualised the sweat pouring off their foreheads, down their shirt collars and flowing from their arm pits down into the innermost parts and onwards into the soles of their boots. At the Depot, it could have been anyone of us who had made a mistake and been in their position;

still I thought that their Extra Drills were better than being shot at dawn and I was glad that I was off to play football.

On that Saturday Rod Graham had a food parcel sent for his birthday and as we had won our match 4-nil, we celebrated with Rod's goodies before going to the NAAFI in the evening. It did help to cheer up Albert Smith who had that morning received a 'Dear John' from his girlfriend who had found someone else to spend time with on a more regular basis.

'Didn't like her much anyway,' said Albert.

'Naw! We we're no too keen on her either.' we retorted. Albert looked at us, burst out laughing, held up his glass of beer and shouted, 'Cheers lads.'

'Cheers Albert.' we all replied as we emptied our glasses and looked about to see whose round it was next.

Breakfast on Sunday morning was sharp and we checked each other over as we waited outside the barrack room to be marched to church. The Padre had a good Scot's accent and his sermon always came across as understanding our situation of being away from home and our loved ones. There was usually a touch of humour about Guard's discipline which sometimes raised an eyebrow from the staff who attended with their families but always a smile from the body of the Kirk which was ourselves. I'm not sure if the Roman Catholics in the squad had a similar laugh from their priest but there was never any hint of discrepancies over the religion that one had chosen to follow.

After dinner we were allowed to walk around and through the Camp in uniform enjoying the afternoon sunshine, having a good old blether and comparing notes when we met lads from the other regiments; some we hadn't seen since the days in the Receiving Room. We were always a little homesick when families, loved ones and visitors were around but food parcels and goodies often appeared afterwards which were shared out and most welcomed. The Depot was a bit too far for most of the families of the Scots and Irish lads to travel but it was enjoyable and peaceful to have a bit of sanity on a Sunday afternoon.

The Passing Out Inspection and our week's leave was gradually moving closer and how we were going to spend that leave was always being discussed. We were now the senior squad in K Company and took a pride in the way we carried ourselves around the Depot, setting the standards for the junior squads and the new recruits whom we were delighted to assist with any queries that they had.

Photos

Church Parade
Dressed for walking out on a Sunday
at Guards Depot, Caterham.
August 1959.
Recruit Gee far left.

Recruit Gee
Guards Depot, Caterham, Surrey
1959

Kit layout for inspection
1959

Some members of the team.
Guards Depot, Caterham.
Inter-company athletic team
Championships winners (us)
K Coy Scots Guards
1959

Recruits in training at the Guards Depot, Caterham, Surrey.
Howard: 2nd row, 2nd from left.

Winners of the Guards Training Battalion
Boxing Championship, Pirbright
L Coy. Scots Guards, 1960

A very smart Regimental Sergeant Major
Guards Depot
1959

Howard ready for war.

P.T Course Nº. 73
Eastern Command School of PT
Shorncliffe, Kent
7/Apr/1960

Easter Command School of P.T.
Shorncliffe, Kent.
April 1960
Howard inspecting the lawn.

Cross country race, 1960.
Howard at Pirbright Camp.
Going for the finish line.
Weather conditions bleak.
200 ran.

March 12th 1960
Preparing for funeral: coffin bearer at Crystal Palace
for ex-Sergeant Major.
Taken at Pirbright Camp.
L Company.

Guards Depot, Pirbright.
P.T. Staff 1960

Howard 1962.
Going on parade in London.

Howard 1962.
London.
Preparing for parade.

Howard and Carmine
22nd April 1961
Edinburgh

Chapter 11 - Farewell To Caterham

'Well,' said Sgt Rudd our Superintendent Sergeant, one morning as we formed up for morning parade on the square. 'the time has come to have a squad photograph taken, show yourself off in your best uniforms and let mummy see what you have been up to these past weeks. The question is are you ready for it?'

'Yes Sergeant.' We shouted unanimously.

'Good,' he said, 'you will be wearing full battle dress, not shirt sleeve order, forage caps, not berets, web belt but no gaiters, tie and shirt with pressed collar and best gleaming boots. Squad Leaders Thomson and Drummond, you will draw up rifles and sit with them between your knees either side of the front rank. The Company Second in Command Captain Scotter who is standing in for the Company Commander, L/Sgts Bath and Park will be in the photograph along with Trained Soldier Woods, and I don't want to hear any derogatory comments thank-you. You will be dressed immaculately, you will not smile in the photograph but you will look happy. Be on parade outside the block at 1415 hours. Do I make myself clear?'

'Yes Sergeant.' we replied and that was that. It was a lovely afternoon and the foliage of some nearby trees provided an excellent backdrop to our photograph which most of us did send home.

We were now carrying out guard duties and practising double sentry drill assimilating public duties at Buckingham Palace, Kensington Palace and the Tower of London whilst rehearsing daily for our Passing Out inspection which the Commandant of the Depot and the Regimental Sergeant Major who both happened to be Scots Guards would personally be on Parade.

Although usually by now we were able to have our kit cleaned to standard well before shining parade finished but as the big day drew nearer we seemed to voluntarily spend longer blancoing webbing, brushing berets and forage caps, polishing boots, pressing uniforms, cleaning brasses and practising standing to attention and saluting in front of full length mirrors. The senior squads of the other regiments would be having their Final Inspection on the same morning and the Commandant would take a salute of the successful squads as they marched passed him and off the square.

'Tomorrow afternoon at 1500 hours' said Sgt Bath, 'the Company Commander will be interviewing you about your future and employment within the regiment; a second interview will take place after battle training at Pirbright. You will be expected to join the battalion and do a tour of public duties before branching out to other specialist fields of employment such as various general infantry duties, mortars, support, supplies, driving and even cooking. Those who wish to jump out of planes may be selected into our Guards Independent Parachute Company. Recruits over six feet tall will go to Right Flank; those of medium height will join left flank and those of a smaller height will go to G Company. Listen to what Major Nicholson asks you, speak up and answer clearly. Do not waffle, don't bother telling him what he doesn't want to know and don't go into detail about what he already knows. Is that clear?'

'Yes Sergeant,' the reply rolled off our tongues as we tried to take in what he had said but knew that we would confer later.

We were marched by the Company Sergeant Major into the Company Commander's office one at a time where we saluted and stood to attention in front of his large desk draped in Royal Stewart tartan.

'Recruit Gee sir,' I said.

'Well now Recruit Gee, you seem to have settled in well to army life. Are you enjoying it?'

'Yes sir.'

'What part of training are you enjoying most?'

'Physical training and sports sir.'

'I thought that's what you might say. I have been hearing good reports about you from your instructors and I believe that you are the youngest in your squad by a few years.'

'Yes sir.' I said my heart sinking in case I was about to be back squaded.

'Perhaps after some training courses you would like to become involved in physical training. Lance Sergeant Park seems to think that you would be successful in that field. You would have to prove that you are worthy of being promoted to Junior Non Commissioned Officer rank. What's your response to that?'

'Great sir, I'd love it. Thank- you sir.'

'Well, we will see how your training develops.' he said as he looked at the Company Sergeant Major and nodded his head.

'Recruit Gee,' said Company Sergeant Major Dempster; 'salute, turn to your right and march out; left, right, left, right, left, right,' and out through the office door I went almost knocking over Bruce Hall waiting to be marched in.

I felt really good but I couldn't take it all in, and anyway, I didn't have time to think about it. I knew that leave was coming up and I did sleep well that night.

Over the next few days our training was geared towards the Inspection and in anticipation of the squad passing, leave passes were filled out and handed into the company clerk in the office where return travel warrants would be completed to destinations as requested.

The day arrived and everyone was up washed and shaved even before the strains of the pipes heralded in reveille. Wearing PT shoes to save our boots being damaged, we were among the first into the cookhouse for breakfast and before trained Soldier Woods could chase us out of the barrack room, we were fully dressed and lined up in front of the armoury waiting to sign out our rifles. As we formed up in our squad, we walked around very slowly to ensure that the layers of gleaming polish on our boots didn't crack and peel off. When we did fall in to three ranks in open order, our Trained Soldier with two other Trained Soldiers from junior squads took a rank each and worked their way along from left to right with a brush in one hand, a yellow duster in the other and inspected every man individually from front to back and top to bottom. Each carried a roll of Sellotape in his pocket and when usage was required, a strip was torn off and wound around his hand with the sticky side outwards on the back of his hand and any undesirable specks were touched, stuck to the Sellotape and then disposed of. Our belts, brasses, cap badges and bayonets were gleaming through time spent rubbing on the bluebell cleaner straight from the tin and when dry, rubbing it off with the magic yellow duster.

Sergeant Rudd and Sergeant Bath arrived, and after an inspection, we were stood at ease whilst given a few words of advice.

'Keep calm and stay switched on.' said Sgt Rudd. 'Listen to Sgt Bath's commands and do not be distracted by anything happening around you on the square. I know that you have worked hard and that you are ready for the Inspection. I will be on the square with 2Lt. Pemberton-Smyth. I will now hand you over to Sgt Bath. Do not let him down. Good luck.'

Sgt Bath gave the order to fix bayonets. 'Do you feel ready to pass?' he asked.

'Yes Sergeant.' we shouted.

'Then you are. The sun is shining for us and it is now up to you. We will march slowly up to the edge of the square and halt before marching on. Stand to attention now and turn to your right. Keep your dressing by the right and we'll march forwards slowly.'

'Right!' said Sgt Bath on reaching the square. 'Stand still and stand at ease. If you want to blow your nose, scratch your crotch or adjust your forage cap, now is the time. If you want to pee, you're too late and don't you dare wet your socks and boots. We will be given the signal by the Inspecting Officer to march on and until then, relax but do not move nor switch off. For your interest there is also a squad from the Grenadier Guards and one from the Coldstream Guards on their Final Inspection this morning but I have no doubt that you already knew that from the NAAFI grapevine.'

'Right, they are now ready for us.' shouted Sgt Bath. 'Brace up; squad, squad shun. By the right, quick march.' and off we went on to the square in the direction of the group of Inspecting Officers spread out and watching our every movement. As the third Regiment of the Line, we were the third to be inspected and as the other squads had been marched off in an orderly manner with heads held high, passed the Commandant on the saluting dais we presumed that they had passed and the pressure was now on us.

We were brought to a halt, formed up in three ranks in open order and watched as the Inspecting Officers approached. There was an Irish and a Welsh Guards Officer assisted by a Grenadier Drill Sergeant.

'K Company squad is ready for your inspection sir.' said Sgt Bath stepping forward to meet and salute the Senior Officer who informed him that they would now inspect the squad. Each rank was inspected for the tiniest detail out of place and the Drill Sergeant carried a mill board writing down all comments as made.

The senior officer, who was a major, then asked Sgt Bath to take us through a nominated series of drill movements which included changing on the march from quick to slow time, saluting with rifles, fixing and unfixing bayonets and marching forward in review order. We were finally brought to a halt when Regimental History questions were asked and answered by individuals. When the Inspecting Officers went into a huddle, we were stood at ease. Sgt Bath was called over and informed by Major O'Hara that the Inspecting Team would like to see again our changeover from the quick march to the slow march which was not an easy drill movement.

Sgt Bath stood in front of us and without moving his head made individual eye contact with the whole squad. 'We are nearly there.' he said. 'Listen to my change of command from the quick march, to slow march. Slam your right foot into the ground and shoot your left foot forward with a straight leg and toe of your boot leading, shoulders back and head up, just as we have practised so many times. Do you all understand me?'

'Yes sergeant.'

'Right,' he said, 'shake off your nerves; let's do it.', and we did and passed the Inspection

'The Commandant and the Regimental Sergeant Major wish to congratulate you on a splendid performance,' said 2Lt Pemberton Smyth 'and the Commandant will take the salute as you march off the square. The Pipe Major from the Piping School has a piper standing by to march you off past the saluting dais to 'Heilan Laddie'.'

'Hold your heads up,' said Sgt Bath, 'arms shoulder high and dig your heels in. As you pass the Commandant look him in the eye and show him that you are proud to be Scots Guards and members of his regiment.' That moment in time was one that we all agreed we would never forget, and when our instructors accepted our invitation to join us at the NAAFI later in the evening for a few celebratory pints of beer, we all joined in with a hearty cheer. We had chipped in and presented each of our instructors with an engraved silver tankard which we had bought through the NAAFI retail shop. As the evening rolled by the thought of packing all our kit into the Quartermaster's stores and going home on leave the following day, was a justifiable reason for a few more pints of beer.

The following morning, we were informed that Major Nicholson wanted to address us outside the Company Office at 0900 hours.

'Congratulations on your inspection.' he said. 'I have been informed that you had one of the highest scores ever and that you are a credit to all your instructors, especially Sgt Rudd and L/Sgt Bath. I know how much you are looking forward to going on leave tomorrow but I have to inform you now that due to unforeseen circumstances your leave has been indefinitely postponed.

'What did he say?' I asked myself.

'There are terrible fires raging on the Surrey Heath near Pirbright and the Local authorities have requested military assistance in the form of vehicles and manpower to extinguish and bring a halt to the fires. You are now required to change into denims; pack all your kit into your kitbags and large packs, keep your helmets on top and be formed up with your kit on the square at 1100 hours when you will leave for the Training Battalion at Pirbright. The other regiments who passed their inspection yesterday have also had their leave postponed and will be travelling down to Pirbright as part of the convoy. Gentlemen it has been a pleasure to have been your Company Commander and I have no doubt that we will meet again within the Regiment. Your training at the depot has now finished and may I wish you all the very best for your Battle Training which will be starting shortly and for the life ahead of you as Scots Guardsmen. Well done to you all.'

We said goodbye to Trained Soldier Woods and thanked him for his help and guidance, and as we shook hands individually with Sgt Rudd and Sgt Bath before climbing on to the waiting three tonners, I looked around at what had been my home for the last twelve weeks and knew that I had changed and nearly matured from the young lad that had entered the Depot gates from civilian life. Remembering the bus driver's comments as we approached the Depot on the morning of my arrival, I decided that I had chosen the right gates.

Chapter12 - Welcome To Pirbright

Unlike the Guards Depot at Caterham, the Guards Training Battalion at Pirbright did not have a perimeter wall and at first glance seemed to be a sprawling area of wooden huts dominated by two large drill squares, a few drill sheds and a number of live firing ranges close by. Each regiment of the Guards had their own Company Offices as did the Independent Guards Parachute Company whose role as pathfinders for the British Army was to lead the way into war zones. The All Arms Drill Wing organised courses for regiments stationed all over the world that sent their Senior Non Commissioned Officers to train and pass out as drill instructors before returning to teach drill within their own regiments. The Junior Guards Company recruited young lads leaving school to join up as Boy Soldiers before transferring into man service at seventeen and a half years of age. They drilled with Mk.4 rifles and had their own Junior and Senior NCOs including their own Junior RSM. New barracks were currently being built which would accommodate a battalion from the Brigade of Guards.

As the vehicles pulled into Pirbright they veered off to their respective company lines and we jumped out at L Company Scots Guards. Before we could even stretch our legs, a company sergeant major, a sergeant and a lance corporal were shouting at us to get sorted out and formed up in three ranks for inspection by the Company Commander, Major Philipson who arrived in a sparkling silver Bentley accompanied by his boxer dog Bandy.

'Welcome to L Company,' he said on his arrival. 'I trust that you had a comfortable journey down here .There is nothing like travelling in the back of a three tonner to shake up the system.' He was of medium height, immaculate in his dress and like many Guards Officers had an air of superiority with an ability to express himself in a quiet manner supported by a well-spoken accent. His brown shoes and Sam Brown (leather belt and cross strap) were gleaming which portrayed the quality work of his batman who was responsible for cleaning and ensuring that all his uniforms were pressed, shirts ironed, belts and shoes were highly polished and all items of personal kit and equipment were looked after and that his officer was turned out for parade literally as a shining example to his men. Major Philipson's limp was due to an extra piece of equipment that he carried and that was his wooden leg. The word was that his Bentley car had been involved in an accident in which he had lost his natural leg. His current batman had now learned to clean, change and fit on to different shoes according to the function or the occasion his new leg. To the delight of the Scots Guards, the authorities in the Ministry of Defence had decided to allow him to continue his career and the row of medals worn on his chest confirmed a good decision had been made.

'You are aware that your leave has been postponed to allow you to assist the local fire brigades to contain and extinguish the fires burning up on the Heath.' he said. 'I know that you understand the situation and will uphold the good name of the Regiment. I will now pass you back to Company Sergeant Major Neill who will explain the programme for the rest of the day.', and returning the CSM's salute, he walked off supported by his sturdy stick and Bandy in the direction of the Officer's Mess.

'Right!' said CSM Neill, 'stand at ease and prick up your ears. On my left is Sergeant Hunt and on my right is Lance Corporal Gray. When you have placed your kit into your accommodation, you will report to the Quartermaster's store, draw up your bedding and get yourselves sorted out. Sgt Hunt, take over and make sure that the platoon is ready for action tomorrow at 0800 hours sharp.'

'Yes sir.' he replied coming to attention. 'You heard the Company Sergeant Major's instructions. Make sure that you are over in the dining room for 1230 and report to the Briefing Room Hut 12 for 1400hrs when I will update you on the situation of the fires up on the Heath and brief you for our early start tomorrow when we will be assisting the fire brigade and local volunteers. Any questions? No? Good. Oh one other thing, don't think that because you have passed out from the Depot that you can now slouch about. You will continue to march around in your platoon as per Scots Guardsmen; head up, arms shoulder high and make sure that those who are to be called sir are called sir and those who are to be saluted are saluted. Lance Corporal Gray and I will be watching your every move. Do I make myself clear?'

'Yes sergeant.'

'Right then, make sure that you have all your kit off the wagon and follow me to your barrack room. Get your bed spaces sorted out before dinner. Stand to attention and on my word of command, turn to your right and fall out.'

At 1355hrs, we were seated in the briefing room and at 1400hrs Sgt Hunt pulled down a map of the Surrey Heath which had the main troubled areas sectioned off.

'Tomorrow morning at 0800hrs sharp, the trucks will be leaving for the Heath. Make sure that you are aboard. Dress is denims, boots and berets. Small packs are to be carried and make sure that you collect your packed lunches at breakfast. On arrival at your designated area, you will be given full instructions as to how to use the poles with asbestos flaps on the end which are to be used for beating out the flames. Do not under any circumstances wander off on your own as a change of wind direction could quite easily cause you to be cut off, resulting in you going up in smoke throwing out the numbers that rations have been allocated for. Do you get my meaning?'

'Yes sergeant.'

'Your main task will be to beat the smouldering brush, preventing any flames from igniting again after having been extinguished. Any questions?'

'What time do we finish sergeant?' asked someone at the back of the squad.

'When you are told to stop work and climb back aboard the trucks and not before.' answered Sgt Hunt. 'Is that clear?'

'Oh yes Sergeant, thank-you.' said the voice and we all smiled.

'Now you may fall out; get your rooms cleaned, kit ready for the morning and have a couple of pints at the NAFFI but do not have a drop more. See you all in the morning. Do not let me down.'

'We won't Sergeant. Sweet dreams.' said the comedian again but keeping his head down out of sight to prevent identification.

Sgt Hunt recognised the sense of humour and appreciated the spirit in the platoon which was an asset in tackling the task ahead. He smiled.

The following morning with all aboard, the vehicles left Pirbright at 0800hrs and headed for the Heath where we were met by the Senior Officer of the fire brigade on site who was controlling the exercise and giving out the instructions and the location that we were to be responsible for under Sergeant Hunt. It was a long day and by 1200hrs our arms and legs were starting to ache with beating the brush. Our faces and hands were black but as we climbed back on to the vehicles at 1630hrs, the feeling of carrying out a worthwhile, responsible task, encouraged an inner feeling of pride and kept an ongoing laughter and loud conversation flowing aided by the inevitable humour in the back of the trucks. After showers and a hearty meal, our denims were brushed down, all our washing done and hung up to dry, kit and equipment cleaned before we headed to the NAFFI for a couple of pints of Brown Ale which were a welcomed asset to a good night's sleep.

For three days, we tackled the smouldering heath and on returning to barracks on the Wednesday evening, Major Philipson was waiting for us. 'Congratulations,' he said. 'You have done the name of the Regiment proud and although the task is not yet complete another Company will move into your section tomorrow morning'.

'You will spend tomorrow, Thursday, sorting yourselves and your kit out as well as drawing up your leave passes from the Company Clerk. On Friday you are going home. Once again, well done, enjoy your leave and I will see you when you return from leave. Carry on Company Sergeant Major.'

'Yes sir.' was the reply as he stood to attention and saluted the Company Commander who returned the salute and left the Company Lines.

There was a silence as the whole platoon continued to stand to attention and look to their front. 'Stand at ease.' came the command from Company Sergeant Major Neill 'You may now smile in a regimental manner.' We burst out laughing and gave three cheers to the Company Commander who was just entering his Office under the veranda of the office block when he stopped turned, smiled and saluted again.

'Right quiet!' came the CSM's voice 'and pin back your ears. You will be travelling home in uniform. You will not be travelling home at all if when you are inspected and your battledress is not pressed to the highest standard, your shirt collar and tie are not ironed, your belt and gaiters are not blancoed, your brasses are not clean, your boots are not gleaming with toe caps like mirrors. Your hat is to be brushed as per regimental custom, dicing cleaned, peak polished and most important of all, your Scots Guards cap badge is to be shining like a beacon of light for all to see. In fact you will not be travelling home at all, if I'm not in a good mood. Your Platoon Sergeant will be around all day tomorrow to deal with any problems that you cannot resolve within the platoon. Early lunches are laid on for Friday and the three tonners will leave at 1300 hours to take you to Brookwood Station. The early departure will allow you to reach Kings Cross for the evening trains to Scotland. I am of course assuming that you are all going home to your waiting anxious mums and cuddly girlfriends. You are not spending the week in the dens of iniquity up in the Smoke are you?'

'No sir.'

'Good,' he said, 'I don't want any poxy diseases spread around my Company when you return. All kit is to be carried in your issued suitcases; do draw up enough funds from the bank in the camp and ensure that your Identity Card and wallet are kept in a safe place on your person. Bedding is not to be handed in to the Quartermaster's store but your bed is to be made down as per sleeping order. Your personal kit and equipment is to be secured in your locker which is to be padlocked, your bed space cleaned and the whole room swept, polished and bumpered before you close and secure the room door. Do I make myself clear?'

'Yes sir.'

'Any questions?'

'No sir.'

Well have a good leave, enjoy the tranquillity of civilian life and oh, in case you haven't yet noticed the dates on your leave passes have been extended by the Company Commander who has granted you an extra two days leave allowing you to travel back on the Monday. Make sure that you are back by 2359 hours as per the date stamped on your leave pass and be ready to start battle training.' We looked at each other, before breaking out with three cheers for Major Philipson.

On Friday after lunch we were inspected prior to boarding the vehicles which rolled out of Pirbright with an excited platoon of Scots Guardsmen aboard. We stood on the platform at Brookwood Station and cheered as the train pulled in and we alighted and headed to London where we began our different routes home. Those for Glasgow and the west headed to Euston whilst we for Edinburgh, Dundee, Aberdeen and Inverness left from Kings Cross and travelled up the east coast crossing the border at Berwick on Tweed. We had managed to get on the 2200hrs overnight to Edinburgh and somehow had managed to squeeze into one compartment. We laughed and joked, ate sandwiches and drank some cans of beer before reaching into our suitcases to pull out some yellow dusters and start bulling our boots. 'We must be mad.' I said.

'We are.' we all shouted.

'But we will be up to Scots Guards regimental standard when we get off this train.' said Callum Blakie.

'Aye!' we all agreed.

As the train rolled on through the night, we laughed some more until we fell asleep. When we awoke we crawled over each other to get to the gents toilet as required; had another beer and fell asleep again. As the train snaked into Edinburgh on a cold morning around 0700hrs the grey tenement buildings brought a tear to my eye. As Callum and I got off, we waved and shouted back to the lads that we would see them all in a week's time. Callum was going for a tramcar to Leith and I jumped into a taxi to take me home to the Inch, my family and Carmine.

Mum, Dad, my brother Ally and Sister Eleanor were all waiting for me at the front door of number 45 Peveril Terrace as the taxi pulled up and after lots of hugging, cuddling and kissing I was ushered into the house where the smell of bacon and eggs was a much welcomed addition to the homecoming celebrations.

'My how you've grown taller and filled out!' exclaimed mum with a proud smile on her face. 'Put your hat on and give us a good look at you in your uniform. Doesn't he look ever so smart dad?'

'Yes you do son, in fact if you step outside the back door into the garden, I'll take a family photograph.'

'It's only 8am,' said mum. 'Mind the noise for the neighbours. It's Saturday and there might be some still in their beds.'

'Never mind worrying about the neighbours, they all know that Howard is coming home; anyway we want a photograph before Howard takes his uniform off.'

Ally took my hat from off his head where he had been trying it on in front of the mirror and handed it to me which gave me the opportunity to tell everyone that you never hold it by the peak and after giving it a rub with my elbow, I placed it on my head in the correct manner. Stepping back inside after the photographs, I removed my hat, boots, battledress top and tie, slung my braces off my shoulder, undid my shirt top button and we all sat down to breakfast.

'We would have had Carmine over but she is working at the surgery today,' said my mother. 'It seems she is a very good receptionist and the doctor's patients think highly of her. She said to tell you that she would see you later this afternoon.'

After relating stories about life at the Guards Depot probably exaggerating bits here and there, I went upstairs, emptied my suitcase, had a bath and changed into some casual clothes which were still hanging in the wardrobe as I had left them all those months ago when I left to join the army. I was feeling fresh, relaxed and decided to walk up to the doctor's surgery to meet Carmine who finished at 1pm on Saturdays.

As I sat on the garden wall at the front of the house which had the surgery attached, watching the world go by and the patients coming and going, I found myself wondering if Carmine would look different. 'How would she feel about me now?' I asked myself; after all the last time I saw her had been an emotional farewell as I boarded the overnight train to Kings Cross en route to Caterham. As she came out of the house waving cheerio to the doctor's children, I thought that her eyes lit up and a broad smile appeared across her lips. She fell into my arms and I held her tight, kissed her on the cheek and for a moment or two not a word was spoken between us.

'What time did you get home?' she asked.

'Did you miss me?' I asked ignoring her question.

103

'Yes,' she said. 'When do you go back?'

'Ages and ages yet.' I said, holding her hand as we strolled down the road to where she lived in the house directly opposite to where I lived at number 45.

Carmine's mother had died when she was very young, and as her older brother and two sisters had left home to get married and start a family, she had been left to run the family home which meant looking after her elderly grandfather, her uncle and father. She had been studying at Nursing College but owing to her commitments at home, she had been forced to leave the College and had taken up the position of a doctor's receptionist.

'What would you like to do to-night?' I asked.

'How does the cinema and fish and chips when we come out appeal to you? I got paid to day.' she said smiling, reminding us both of the time when we were at school and I had taken her to see the film 'South Pacific' but didn't have enough money to get in, buy some sweets and pay for the bus home. Lucky she had some change in her purse for the bus although we had to ask for halves as school children on that bus going home. The conductor had been very understanding. I reminded her that I was now a member of Her Majesty's Forces and actually had enough money to buy some chocolates on the way in and an ice cream during the interval, if she behaved herself. We both burst out laughing. Carmine was given a few days off by Doctor Thomson who along with Mrs Thomson had made her an almost honorary member of their family and were very grateful when on occasions, she did baby sitting for them.

We spent the days walking in Princes's Street Gardens, Holyrood Park, climbed Arthurs Seat, and strolled around the shops of Edinburgh. Some nights, we danced in the Palais at Fountainbridge, and others we just cuddled up in front of the fire and watched television. We talked about the past and the future; enjoying every moment together; discussing families, our religious beliefs, the joys of life and trying to understand what life held for us whilst confirming that we did want to continue to be together.

The days and nights rolled by so quickly and I again had a lump in my throat saying farewell to Carmine who had a tear in her eye as I boarded the overnight train back to London and on to Pirbright.

Chapter 13 - Battle Training

It was great seeing all the lads again and when we formed up in our platoon the following morning wearing full battle order including helmets, we knew that training had now taken a serious step forward and that we were now well on our way to becoming fully trained soldiers.

Major Philipson with Bandy at his side addressed the platoon and told us exactly what to expect of our training from now on; battle fitness, weapon training skills including the use of the bayonet and close combat self-defence. There would be live firing on the ranges, night exercises where thunder flashes would be used in abundance and lack of sleep would hinder sound decisions whilst patience would be tested with the actions of individual platoon members. Freezing wet conditions when carrying a wounded comrade to safety would require physical stamina and willpower. All kit and equipment was to be kept clean and ready for immediate use when required. Discipline and drill would remain at the highest standard as expected of a Scots Guardsman. 'Oh and by the way,' he said, 'the Inter Company Boxing is coming up shortly and I expect our Company to win. Fitness training will have to be carried out in the early mornings and evenings outside of your military training hours but I don't expect that to be a problem. Do you?'

'No sir.' was the loud response.

'Good,' he said. 'Come Bandy.' he called as he turned and strolled off towards his office which lay at the end of a long wooden veranda.

Company Sergeant Major Neill stepped forward. 'Right!' he said, 'I presumed that you all enjoyed your leave which will be your last if you don't get down to working hard at the training that lies ahead and achieving the standards which the Company Commander expects of you. You are now going for a two mile run followed by a session on the assault course under Lance Corporal Morton, your Scots Guards

Assistant Physical Training Instructor. After dinner you will Blanco all your webbing including your belt and gators, clean your brasses, fit your camouflage net on to your helmet and press your greatcoat ensuring that the creases are sharp on the sleeves and in the small of the back. You will be inspected by Sgt Hunt and L/Cpl Gray at 1545hrs just before we meet in the empty barrack room at the rear of the company lines where the boxing team will be selected from yourselves and the other Scots Guards Platoons in training. Dress PT kit and plimsolls. L/Cpl Gray will ensure that the 8oz.gloves, buckets, sponges, some red and blue sashes and a first aid box are drawn up from the stores. Any questions? No? Over to you Sgt Hunt, and remember all of you, that you are to do your very best to be selected for the team.'

'Right Company Sergeant Major.' replied Sgt Hunt and we were back into the Scots Guards way of life again.

L/Cpl Morton made sure that the challenging pace he set for the run was just enough to have us coughing, spluttering and gasping for breath as we reached the assault course. We started at, and crawled through, the large concrete pipes filled with freezing cold water, held our balance as we walked across the wet slippy logs stretched across the water ditches and helped each other over various walls and obstacles. The rope swings were next and by this time we were left with very little strength to hold on and prevent ourselves from falling into the uninviting morass of mud and water. 'Well done.' encouraged our PT Instructor as we struggled around the course. As the last man came in, we stood to attention in our platoon; our chests heaving up and down as we gulped fresh air into our lungs. 'Well done.' he said again as he looked at his watch. 'You have completed the course in such good time; you now have space in the programme for one more run.' We looked at him to see if he was joking but we should have known better.

'Get ready, go!' and we were off, mumbling under our breath; our boots sliding and sinking into the surrounding heavy mud as we pushed forward on our second run.

We just had time to shower before making our way to the dining room where we almost collapsed as we passed the hotplates and on towards the dining tables, trying to prevent our filled plates from sliding off the trays on to the floor. Our kit was cleaned, pressed and duly inspected at the nominated time. 'The results of the inspection were quite good.' said Sgt Hunt. 'The faults that were picked up must be corrected for the next inspection. Well done. Now go and get into your PT kit and get straight over to the boxing training room.'

'You know your weights.' said L/Cpl Gray, 'Get in line starting around nine stone i.e. all the budding lightweights up to the heavies at the back. Sgt Hunt will record your weight when you step on to the scales. I know that we have some promising champions amongst you and we will find out this afternoon just how good you are.' I weighed in at 11 stone 2 pounds and was chosen for the team in the light middleweight category. After sparring, the team almost picked itself, and it turned out to be a strong team which won the Inter Company Championships to the delight of our Company Commander and I've no doubt Bandy was given some extra doggie biscuits that night.

Loading, firing, unloading, stripping, oiling, cleaning and fitting together again our Rifles (SLRs), Sub Machine Guns and General Purpose Machine Guns (GPMGs) was a priority in the training programme under the auspices of the Weapon Training Staff. Safety drills were carried out at all times especially when firing on the ranges; not only during night exercises but during daylight hours. After searching one's own pockets of all items of clothing and equipment before leaving the range, an individual declaration of 'I have no live rounds or ammunition in my possession sir.' had to be made. The consequences of a live round being found on one's

108

person after leaving the range was a serious matter and dealt with accordingly.

For night exercises, foxholes were dug, faces and hands were blackened and bushes, branches and leaves were used to ensure that we were camouflaged and unseen by oncoming enemy, acted out by various other platoons. Sign language was taught and used to prevent any sounds reaching the enemy in the serenity of the night when personal senses were at their peak. Aftershave, body odours, sprays, hair creams and such delights were banned as human smells could quickly be detected on the slightest breeze. Fires of course could not be lit and one had to ensure warmth by wearing the right clothing as issued. Before leaving barracks, hardtack biscuits with varieties of pre-cooked easily opened tinned food called Compo which had different flavours were often exchanged with one another according to personal choices. Our waterproof capes were invaluable in wet conditions and kept ourselves and our kit dry not to mention being able to cover wet patches on the ground that one had to lie on. At the end of the exercises, before boarding the trucks to return to barracks, we stood around a large bonfire, drank mugs of tea and talked about the experience of that night. After drying and cleaning our kit, equipment and weapons, we had a few hours sleep in the warmth of our beds before the dawn was creeping in and reveille sounded for another day.

On Saturday mornings the whole Training Battalion was on parade under the control of the Regimental Sergeant Major and Drill Sergeants. Company Commanders were present and Platoon Officers were active pacing up and down the square whilst pipers and the military band provided the music for the march past and the salute to the Commanding Officer. In the afternoon extra drills were held for those who had not been up to standard on the parade whilst the lucky ones were selected to play sports. I was delighted to be picked for the company rugby, cross country and basketball teams and every spare minute I had seemed

109

to be used up in playing sports but I was enjoying the life. The days and weeks rolled by and the leaves had now fallen off the trees as summer had slipped into autumn which changed into winter. Warmer underwear including long johns, jumpers and gloves were now being worn. One evening, Company Memorandum stated that all Scots Guardsmen would be expected to attend the Saint Andrews Ball to be held in the gymnasium on the Friday nearest the 30th November when the 1st.Batallion Pipes and Drums would be present along with the Brigade of Guards Military Band. The Dance Orchestra which was a section of the Military Band would provide the dance music throughout the evening. All Officers, Warrant Officers and their ladies, Senior and Junior NCOs and their wives and all ranks with the women of their choice and guests are invited and to be made welcome. Two coaches will bring single, female guests into the camp and the same coaches will return all such guests from the camp at the end of the evening to their designated areas from which they came.

On the night of the ball, the Regimental Police ensured that most who attended did behave and any who didn't, especially through too much drink, spent the night in the cells, allowing everyone else to have an enjoyable evening. The dress for gents was blazers and flannels, jackets or suits; ties as always were to be worn. Most of our platoon started at the bar ogling the talent and after a couple of rounds found a long table to sit around; drinking, laughing, getting merry, enjoying the atmosphere and the music whilst singing heartily to the Scottish tunes being played by the pipe band as they marched up and down the gymnasium. As the night wore on, words became more slurred, eyelids struggled to remain open and as 0100 hrs approached, last orders were again called and there was a further surge to the bar. It had been a long day for us and most of us slowly made our way down the hill to our room and our beds. The night exercises had began to take their toll.

Next morning our platoon had been detailed for cleaning up after the ball which entailed a host of duties including gathering all the empty bottles and placing them into crates at the bar. Flags and decorations were taken down and stored away, tables and chairs were stacked ready for collection, the gymnasium floor was scrubbed, wall bars washed and dusted, gymnasium mats and equipment returned from storage and all training areas made ready for physical training first thing on Monday morning. A lost and found property office was established and was sure to be busy once the sobering up period had begun. As always Sunday followed Saturday and after Church Parade a day of rest was called for or rather a day of recovery.

Our programme for Monday contained a day of various activities, starting with a run wearing full battle kit, followed by grenade throwing, use of the bayonet and close quarter combat skills. As we marched up to the gymnasium, it was obvious to L/Cpl Gray that the whole platoon was still recovering from having had more than their fair share from the bar on the Friday night. When he suggested to L/Cpl Morton to take us on a three mile run to warm us up, the groans could have been heard by the Padre down at the church, although if we were lucky I thought to myself, he might find the time to say a small prayer to help us on our way. Although we finished the run as a platoon back at the gymnasium, a few threw up, some collapsed on to their backs and some just stood bent over on their wobbly legs trying to gulp as much air into their heaving lungs as possible. 'I'm glad you all had such a good night at the ball and remembered about training this morning.' sneered L/Cpl Gray. 'Now get formed up in your platoon and we'll go over to the grenade throwing range at the rear of the assault course. Just be glad that you are not doing close combat first where you might be thrown up in the air, do a loop the loop and end up on your back. Thankyou Cpl Morton, I'll take them over to their next lesson. By the right double march.' and off we went with a sigh of relief that the run was behind us.

We were shown by L/Cpl Gray how to hold and throw dummy grenades in various directions, over high and

111

low wires and obstacles from all sorts of positions such as standing, kneeling and lying down not to mention around corners. 'Just remember to let go when you have pulled out the pin,' shouted L/Cpl Gray, 'or your friends in the platoon, if there are any still standing, will be sweeping and shovelling you up out of respect. You now have fifteen minutes of free practice to improve your throwing skills before lunch which will be brought out to you in dixies today so that we don't have to waste time going to the cookhouse. Hope you all brought your eating irons for the stew and mugs for the tea.'

'Yes corporal.' was the reply.

'Get formed into three sections,' was the command as we reached the bayonet practice area, 'and remember all that you have been taught about safety when handling the bayonet.'

We fixed bayonets and ran up and down the runs screaming as we stabbed heavy sacks which were swinging between wooden posts or lying on the ground representing the enemy. Sgt Hunt who had now joined the instructors with 2/Lt Trembleton was shouting at us to 'lunge, thrust and twist' the bayonet before withdrawing it and running on towards the next target. Posts got knocked over, bayonets got stuck in the targets and Donald Gunn nearly got Rab MacAlistair's bayonet right up his rear end when Donald's bayonet got stuck in a sack and he was bent over determined to pull it out. The language directed at us by the instructors was quite clear as to where they thought the bayonets should go but it all sounded very normal to us by now.

'The food has arrived,' said Sgt Hunt, 'break off now for dinner before we proceed to close combat.'

'That was a close shave, Donald,' I said. 'I was trying to picture you arriving at the Medical Centre with a ....'

'With a bayonet right up your arse,' said Pete McKinlay who couldn't help butting in.

'Why don't we just shoot the enemy from a distance?' mumbled Donald as we stood in the queue for food.

'Aye,' we all agreed, 'a good idea Donald.'

When lunch break was over, we made our way to the clearing where a Sergeant Instructor wearing the badge of the Guards Independent Parachute Company in his red beret and an SAS badge on his arm, taught us how to deal with an armed enemy advancing towards us with a knife when we ourselves had no weapon. 'Look him in the eyes,' he said, 'adapt an aggressive stance, block with your forearm his raised attacking hand holding his knife, kick him in the crutch and follow through with a chop to the side of the neck.' Different directions of attacks with various weapons were demonstrated and dealt with in unexpected ways but always ended with the attacker disarmed and totally out of action. Although we appreciated that only practice would make us perfect, we all enjoyed the lesson and thanked the instructor for teaching us new skills and installing a new self-confidence into us.

Right said Sgt Hunt, take a few swigs from your water bottle and get into your sections again. Cpl Morton is waiting to brief you on the assault course.

'Don't rush the course.' said Cpl Morton. 'Be careful balancing and traversing the wet logs and rope bridges. Prior to scaling the high netting, sling you rifle over your back. When jumping the ditches, bend both knees, keep your feet together and on landing at the other side, dig the butt of your rifle into the ground to help you maintain your balance; the butt I said, not the muzzle. Clear the 6ft.wall quickly and help each other over the 12ft wall as you were shown last week. Traversing the logs across the water ditches, keep your rifles slung across your back and do not fall in. Adapt the leopard crawl through the tunnels holding your weapon in your hands in front of the body and use your elbows alternately to manoeuvre your way through as you push with the sides and soles of your boots. Do not stop for breath and get back here without getting injured. Do I make myself clear?'

'Yes corporal.' was the loud reply.

'Right off you go then.' he shouted and off we went oblivious to anything else happening in the world. Needless to say some fell into the muddy cold slimy water and stood shivering at the end but all completed the course with a few sprains, twisted knees, bumps, knocks and other minor injuries, although a few plasters and bandages were taken out of the first aid packs to cover the bleeding of some relatively small cuts. Strapping was wrapped around bruised thumbs, sore muscles were rubbed and general aches and pains were mumbled about which made everyone feel better.

At the end of the afternoon, we returned to the huts, had showers and changed for tea after which we settled down to a night of washing our clothes, cleaning and brushing our kit and equipment, blancoing our webbing, polishing and bulling our boots. Our underwear, socks and all other wet items of clothing were dried, ironed and made ready for training again, first thing in the morning. At 1900 hours, L/Cpl Gray announced that we could have a 20 minute break to go to the NAFFI and buy some food and drinks but that we had to bring it back to the hut to scoff as we carried on with our cleaning tasks which is what we did. I had just unwrapped a large warm steak pie and laid it on my bed, the mouth-watering aroma spreading throughout the room when the door opened and in walked Major Philipson with Bandy. Jim Drummond one of the Squad Leaders called us to attention and to stand by our beds.

'I have been informed that you had a hard day today and that you worked well as a team.' said Major Philipson. 'I hope that you enjoyed your training today and felt that it was valuable and worthwhile. Well done to you all, enjoy your supper and have a good night's sleep. Good night,' he called as he stepped out of the door followed by Bandy.

It was only at that point when I glanced down at my bed, I realised that my steak pie was missing and Bandy was walking out the door slavering at the mouth. After we all had a good laugh I was allowed to run over to the NAFFI and replenish my supper.

Chapter 14 - A Trained Scots Guardsman

'Tomorrow morning, you will require your respirators for your induction to dealing with escaping gas,' said Sergeant Hunt, 'and I would strongly advise you all not to have a large breakfast. L/Cpl Gray will carry out room inspection at 0800 hrs and I will meet you at 0830 hrs outside the gas chamber.'

'Sounds fun.' said Albert Smith.

'You must have had a dull life.' I retorted. 'We had a gas poker that helped to light the fire on freezing cold mornings before we went to school. We didn't exactly enjoy life shivering whilst getting dressed before we could go out to the toilet which was on the stair landing, and before you ask, aye it was outside the house and we did share it with the neighbours.'

'Listen in.' shouted L/Cpl Gray. 'This could be a painful experience if you don't react properly and quickly enough to the gas. It might be what you would call a crying matter.' he said, looking around for a laugh which didn't come. We had all heard of the experience from platoons who had completed this part of training and although their stories may have been a little exaggerated there was something harrowing about their tales especially in relation to prisoners in the German concentration camps which had been handed down through the platoons.

'Good morning.' called Sgt Hunt as he approached the platoon. 'I trust that you all slept well and had a hearty breakfast, he said with a smile stretching across his face.

'Good morning Sergeant.' was the response but remembering what we had been told about not eating a full breakfast before this exercise, there was no further comment from us.

I think Sgt Hunt understood. 'Right let's get started.' he said.

'Form a half circle in front of me and we'll go through the drill again which we practiced last week. Pin back your ears and listen carefully. Check that your respirators are firmly in their holders which should be resting securely on your hip. When I shout the warning, gas, gas, gas, take them out and place them on to your face pulling the straps upwards and over your head. When they are firmly on, place your hands by your side. If you are having difficulty, put your hand in the air and L/Cpl Gray or myself will come to help you. Ready? Gas, gas, gas.' he shouted and respirators were immediately extracted from their holders and pulled on.

'Not bad but some of you were a bit slow and would be dead by now.' said Sgt Hunt. 'We'll try again but this time you can help the man to your left if he's having difficulty but only after you have fitted your own respirator on properly. Gas, gas, gas.' he shouted again. 'That was better but one or two of you were still a bit slow. You have got to pull the straps over your head, adjust the front of the respirator and fit it on to your face quicker. Remember do not try to help anyone else until you are sure that your own respirator is on and you are breathing properly. Any Questions? No! Then let's go for it.' said Sgt Hunt pulling open the huge metal door of the round concrete building and ushering us inside.

'Stand with your backs to the wall looking inwards.' ordered L/Cpl Gray. 'I will remain inside by the door. You must remember if you are in trouble to raise your hand. There is a medical sergeant outside if required but I don't think that you will need him.' The huge metal door slammed shut and there was a deathly silence in the dim light as claustrophobia crept silently around touching individuals. Nobody said a word. Everyone glanced at each other wondering what was to follow when suddenly two grenades of smoking gas were thrown in to the room through a small slot high up on the wall and landed on the floor.

'Gas, gas, gas.' shouted L/Cpl Gray and we all went into action; pulling on our respirators. I pulled mine on and checked Malcolm MacRae to my left and he gave me the thumbs up but across the room Hamish MacPherson had dropped to his knees trying to pick up his respirator which had fallen to the ground and Murdoch MacLeod was trying desperately to pull the strap over his head but it was sticking somewhere between his chin and his ears. Both were coughing and spluttering as tears were streaming from their eyes and rolling down their cheeks when L/Cpl Gray hammered the pre-arranged signal on the door which eased open and the two distressed lads were dragged outside by helping hands into the fresh air before the door slammed shut again. After a few minutes the door was opened and we were ushered outside. 'Take your respirators off and go and sit on the grass. Relax and take some deep breaths of fresh air into your lungs.' shouted Sgt Hunt. 'The Medical Sergeant has checked out our two stalwarts, bathed their eyes and has reported that they are ready to go back in. Go over and talk quietly to them and give them a bit of encouragement.'

'MacPherson and MacLeod,' shouted L/Cpl Gray, 'you have ten minutes left before you go back in and get it right this time.' which they did and received a big cheer from the platoon when they came out.

'Well done to all of you.' said 2LtTrembleton who had turned up to see how we had done. 'I know that this part of training will always stick in your minds if not your throats.'

'Yes sir.' we shouted, forcing a smile.

That afternoon we were back running around the assault course having been divided into teams with each team carrying a large log. Exercises were then carried out by raising the logs in the air through stretching and bending the arms, holding and pushing the logs away from our bodies and pulling them back; standing astride the logs, lifting them up and running with them between our legs. We finished with a relay race where the last man lay flat on top of an upright log with his arms and legs outstretched in a star position whilst his team supported the log. It was competitive, very hard on the arm muscles but good fun and some of us loved it.

The old Company huts had been refurbished and the new accommodation was ready to move into. The walls had been painted, coal fire stoves had been replaced by modern radiators, new orange coloured curtains hung up at the windows and where the old wooden floor boards had lain there was now linoleum which could be polished and bumpered easily. The small wooden lockers had been replaced by large metal lockers complete with drawers and mirror and could accommodate twice the amount of personal kit and stored items. The sagging well used mattresses were replaced with foam mattresses which were not only comfortable but had defined box shaped edges which looked impressive on room inspections. New wooden tables and chairs made the room look comfortable and lived in but tidy whilst new large mats at each bed space gave an at-home feeling. The washrooms, toilets, showers and baths had all been refurbished and modernised; rubber plugs were attached with chains to sinks to discourage their removal from the sinks. There were no cracks on walls or windows and doors were fitted properly to ensure that unwelcomed draughts were kept out. Beds either side of the room fitted into their own allotted space and there was a feel good factor at returning to a place of comfort and relaxation at the end of a day's training. Cleaning one's kit, having a conversation and a good laugh, whilst being warm especially as the long, cold, dark, winter nights were creeping in around 1600 hrs raised everyone's spirits.

Mornings were frosty and care had to be taken as we made our way to the cookhouse for breakfast where a welcomed plate of piping hot porridge, a good fry up, some toast and a mug of tea were always ready and waiting for us.

Guard, sentry and stag duties at night were especially cold but at least with the latter we were kept moving around the camp in pairs checking the security

119

of stores and locked buildings; keeping out of the biting wind whenever possible.

Although we hadn't realised it, the physical training both inside and outside the gymnasium was much more strenuous now and we were able to run faster and further carrying an assimilated wounded comrade as required; vault over gymnastic boxes and tumble and roll across mats with ease. We were more agile, stronger and able to climb up ropes and over walls without falling off, swing across wide ditches landing safely on the other side, crawl through dark, narrow tunnels without being claustrophobic, balance walk along logs laid across water ditches and complete rope walks high up in the trees without hesitation when ordered to do so. We were taught to be aware of any lurking dangers; taking the appropriate action as required and all whilst wearing full battle kit and carrying our personal weapons. We were now realising that when we played sports, to win, we had to play as a team. We were all members of a platoon, comrades and friends with whom we had to work together, laugh and socialise but most of all we had to know that we could trust each other and be relied upon when needed.

On the 10th December, I shared out my birthday parcel with the lads and bought a round of drinks at the NAFFI. I had just turned 18 years of age and was enjoying army life.

The dates and times for the Company Commander's Interview were placed on Company Memorandum and there was a real buzz about the platoon although we guessed that most of us would be going to join the 2nd Battalion at Gravesend in Kent. Those over six feet tall would join Right Flank. Those of a medium height would join Left Flank and those of a lesser height were bound for G Company or Headquarter Company but all would be trained up initially to carry out Public Duties at Buckingham Palace, Clarence House, Tower of London, Holyrood Palace in Edinburgh, Braemar in the Highlands and other royal residences as required. All of us would be measured for wearing the scarlet tunics which would be individually tailored. Bearskins had to be fitted, brushed and trimmed regularly whilst their chin straps were adjusted to individual facial features. Double sentry drill between the sentry boxes and the saluting of officers and VIPs whilst carrying rifles required rehearsed precision drill. The senior member of the guard used the butt of his rifle to tap on the ground a number of coded signals for both sentries to carry out the required drill; such as coming to attention at the sentry box and marching up and down which the crowds of visitors loved to watch. After carrying out Public Duties for an allocated period of time, some of the lads would join Support Company perhaps the Mortar Platoon or HQ Company to become drivers, train as clerks, cooks, and regimental medics, work in the Quartermaster's store or carry out other duties within the battalion not to mention the Regimental Police.

'Interviews with the Company Commander are tomorrow morning,' announced Sgt Hunt, 'when you will be informed of your future within the Regiment. Make sure that your uniform is immaculate and your personal drill when you march in and out of his office is of the highest standard. Your Platoon Officer and myself will be present. Listen to what Major Philipson has to say; hold your head up, answer his questions clearly and do not mumble. There is to be no remarks when he tells you where you are posted to. You will be marching in as per alphabetical order except Recruit Gee.'

'Oh no.' I thought to myself. 'What have I done wrong?'

'Gee, you will bring up the rear. Does everyone understand my instructions?'

'Yes Sergeant.' we shouted.

At the NAFFI that night the conversation was all about our interviews the following day and the comments about me going in last were humorous. After a few beers the excitement was forgotten until after breakfast the following morning when we paraded outside the

Company Commander's office and were marched in; one at a time until I was the only one left.

'March in Recruit Gee.' shouted the Company Sergeant Major. 'Left, right, left, right; mark time, halt.' and I came to a halt, dead centre of Major Philipson's desk.

'Stand at ease.' shouted the Sergeant Major and I did with both hands clasped behind my back. Major Philipson looked me up and down before asking if I was enjoying life as a Scots Guardsman.

'Yes sir.' I said.

'You seem to like fitness training and I've noticed that you excel in a number of sports young Gee. Your Physical training instructors both here and at Caterham speak very highly of you although your sense of humour is sometimes suspect, I hear. Your platoon NCOs believe that you have the makings of a good Lance Corporal and would be respected accordingly. Would you like to be sent on a course and trained as an Assistant Physical Training Instructor and be posted back here to the Training Battalion?'

'Yes sir, that would be great sir,' I said trying to take it all in.

'Do you think that you could gain respect of guardsmen who have been in the regiment for a number of years, give out instructions and orders, control anyone who may not be happy with your orders and take the necessary disciplinary action as required whilst carrying out regimental duties and assisting in teaching physical training to new recruits?'

'Yes sir, I'm sure I could sir.' I replied not really understanding what I was agreeing to.

'Then we shall see.' said Major Philipson. 'I will see you again before we go home for Christmas Leave.' I knew that the interview was over when I was called to attention by the CSM, told to salute and turn to my right before being marched out of the office.

We were informed that the following day a Senior Colonel from the Royal Army Pay Corps would be visiting the Training Battalion and would attend the L Company pay parade accompanied by Major Philipson. The senior platoon, which was ourselves, was selected to demonstrate how an efficient pay parade should be held. We were also to be responsible for ensuring that the room was immaculate; windows were clean, curtains were hanging properly, window sills and all ledges were dusted and the floor had a fresh layer of polish laid the night before and bumperd up to the highest standard, first thing in the morning.

'Now remember,' said Sgt Hunt, 'the format will be slightly different from normal. Come to attention when your name is called out by the Pay Corps Sergeant sitting at the table; march forward, halt and salute the Scots Guards Paying Out Officer sitting to his left. As you cut your right hand away from the salute, shoot out your left hand holding your pay book which the sergeant will take, enter the amount due, hand the book to the officer who will sign and place the correct amount of money into the book and hand it back to you. You are to salute, turn to your right and march out of the hut. Do not stop to check that you have the right amount of money until you are outside and back in the platoon. If there has been a mistake, you are to inform me.'

All was going smoothly until the Company Sergeant Major called out 'Recruit Graham.' Rod sprang to attention and marched up to the six foot table, bent his right knee to halt but as his studded boot landed on the floor, it slid on the newly polished linoleum and Rod went sliding under the table which went up in the air, knocking the sergeant and officer backwards off their chairs, scattering all the coins and notes which had been neatly laid out on the table. There was a deathly hush before Major Philipson turned to the CSM and said, 'carry on Company Sergeant Major,' as he ushered the Colonel out of the door. There was a lot of shouting and bawling as we rushed to help Rod, the sergeant and the officer up off the floor, not to mention the money.

'Are you alright sergeant?' asked Lt. Farquharson rising from the floor.

'Yes sir; a pay parade with a difference sir.' he replied.

'Well, Company Sergeant Major,' said Lt. Farquharson, 'as no-one has been hurt shall we have a good laugh and carry on with the Pay Parade?' and we did.

Major Philipson addressed the platoon later that day and said that as nobody could really be blamed for the unfortunate mishap, it was better that we didn't say too much about the matter which had been handled very well by all present. 'Well done to everyone,' he said, 'although Recruit Graham must learn to halt properly in the future'. That night at the NAFFI over a few beers, we had another good laugh about Rod trying to halt under a six foot table.

The night before our Passing Out Parade we sat on our beds, talking, cleaning our kit, shining our brasses and polishing our boots but there was a strange feeling that this could be our last shining parade together unless we failed our drill or inspection on the parade and that just couldn't even be contemplated. The atmosphere in the barrack room was subdued. As every item of uniform was checked and pressed with the creases exactly where they should be, it was carefully laid to one's side or hung up on a coat hanger out of harm's way. Everyone went round helping each other and everyone knew and understood that the pre-inspections by the Platoon Sergeant, Platoon Officer and Company Commander prior to the parade would be the hardest of all. Supper was taken at our bed space as we continued to work on our kit; nothing was going to stop us passing out tomorrow morning.

All the senior platoons from the other regiments were also Passing Out and what a memorable parade it was. The Major General from London in his speech said that he was extremely pleased with the standard of turnout and drill of all platoons and that we were a credit to our instructors and our regiments. He wished us all the very best for our future in the Regiments and said that he was sure that he would meet with us again. 'Have a safe journey home and an enjoyable leave.' he said. 'Good luck for the New Year and the exciting times ahead.' and he finished by taking the salute as the parade marched past.

As each platoon passed the saluting dais, they gave an eyes right to the General as the band played their Regimental March and when the pipes broke into 'Heilan Laddie' we all said afterwards that there had been a lump in our throats. As we left the square for the last time as recruits the band broke into 'Jingle Bells' and 'We Wish You A Merry Christmas'. With our heads held high, shoulders back and our arms swinging shoulder high; we smiled and left the square as Scots Guardsmen. That afternoon the Padre and the Priest visited us, gave us their blessings for the future and asked us to have faith in the Lord wherever our duties would take us and to remember our comrades in their hours of need. We all said that we would and thanked them for being there for us throughout our training.

Later that afternoon the Commanding Officer was touring the camp with the Adjutant and stopped to congratulate the platoon on our standard of drill during the parade. Both wished us all a Merry Christmas.

We started packing our kit to be transferred the following day to the Quartermaster's stores at the barracks in Gravesend where we were to join the 2nd Battalion after Christmas Leave. I was wondering what was happening to me when the Company Clerk informed me that I was to report to the CSM's office immediately. 'Major Philipson wants to see you now.' said the CSM who knocked on the Company Commander's office door, marched me in and stood me at ease in front of the Company Commander.

'Well young Gee, how does it feel to be a Scots Guardsman?' asked the Company Commander.

'Great sir.' I said

'Are you going home tomorrow? Edinburgh I believe.'

'Yes sir.' I replied.

'Well I have to tell you that you are not joining the Battalion with your platoon after Christmas Leave but that you are being posted to the Physical Training Staff here at the Training Battalion'.

'How do you feel about that?'

I was speechless.

'What do you think?' asked the Company Commander

'Just great sir.' I answered.

'Well you will have to wear these, he said, stretching over the desk to hand me two sets of chevrons; one set for each arm. You are now a Lance Corporal and I wish to congratulate you on your promotion. Go and enjoy your leave and come back ready to accept the responsibilities that I have given to you with these chevrons. Can I rely on you to do that?'

'Oh yes sir.' I said trying to take it all in.

'L/Cpl Gee, fall out and wait outside.' said the CSM who came out after a few minutes and shook me warmly by the hand congratulating me on my promotion. 'Tonight,' he said, 'you may drink with your platoon in the NAAFI but when you come back off leave you will socialise in the Corporal's Mess. Is that clear?'

'Yes sir.'

'Right off you go. Keep out of trouble especially tonight. Have a good Christmas. Enjoy your leave and come back ready to be a responsible Junior Non Commissioned Officer, carrying out your duties efficiently and with pride.'

'Thank-you sir; thank-you very much sir.'

That night, the passing out platoons from all the regiments celebrated in the NAAFI and a record number of pints of beer were downed without any of the usual banter between regiments. We were now all members of the Brigade of Guards together and everyone was looking forward to Christmas Leave. Throughout the evening, the lads kept congratulating me on my promotion and standing to attention in a mocking way when speaking to me but when last orders were called and a bit of lenient drinking up time given, we rolled back to the barrack rooms and our warm cosy beds.

The following day was bitterly cold as we left Brookwood Station and climbed aboard the train to London where overnight travel would take us onwards to Scotland. Farewells were again said at Kings Cross as we headed for the trains to Glasgow, Edinburgh and all points north. It was 0600 hours on the 19th of December as I stepped down from the train and left the Waverly Station in Edinburgh. The snow was falling heavily; I pulled my coat collar up and as my fingers curled around my holdall, I was grateful that I was wearing my thick army woollen gloves. I smiled to myself and felt so proud to be a trained Scots Guardsman as I headed home for Christmas.

Chapter 15 - Physical Training

I accompanied Carmine to Midnight Mass on Christmas Eve. On Christmas Day about three o'clock, we sat down around the table and after grace we tucked in to a large chicken and all the trimmings, followed by plum duff pudding and custard, fruit, nuts, sweets and various titbits. Crackers were pulled, games were played and songs were sung accompanied by my dad on the piano. The festivities were great fun and enjoyed by all. New Year celebrations arrived which included the neighbours 'first footing' and amidst music, singing and dancing which seemed to go on forever;1960 swept into our lives all too quickly.

Before I left, I asked Carmine if she would marry me and she said 'Yes.' The following day, we bought an engagement ring and decided that the date of the wedding would be sometime in 1961. Once again I had to say farewell as Carmine waved me off at the Waverly Station, back to the Guards Training Battalion where I was to join the Physical Training Staff.

On my arrival at L Company, CSM Neill informed me that as with immediate effect, I would be the NCO taking over the responsibility of the Permanent Staff Bathack Room and the room next door which was for staff in transit. Not only was I to be responsible for ensuring that the duties of maintenance, cleanliness and security of the rooms were carried out but for ensuring that the staff, the old soldiers, the barrack room lawyers who occupied the rooms did adhere to the required standards as laid down in Regimental Standing Orders. I would now be expected to take disciplinary action as required against guilty culprits who ignored the orders which really meant that I would be the most unpopular person in the room where I myself would have to live.

'Oh no!' I thought to myself. I was to be in charge, make required decisions and follow through with required action, pleasant or otherwise.

'Are you up to it?' asked CSM Neill.

'Yes sir.' I said, knowing it to be the expected answer but not really sure what I was committing myself to or whether I could in fact carry it all out.

'Right Cpl Gee, go and draw up your bedding and sort your bed space out before the members of the rooms return from their places of work. I suggest that you take the bed in the corner nearest the door and you can see who comes and goes. You will have two lockers, three if you can get another from somewhere and make a bit of privacy for yourself in that corner. You must let all personnel in both rooms know that you are now in charge and whilst they have their own space to live and sleep in, your instructions are to be obeyed. I suggest that you tell them that they may approach you at any convenient time to both of you to discuss any problems they may have. Pin up on the notice board a rota of cleaning duties ASP; the Company Clerk will provide you with a nominal role of all who are at present living in the rooms. Oh! and check out that the Fire and Security Orders on the notice board are up to date with current regulations; the Company Clerk will also assist you in doing that. Make sure also that the fire buckets are filled with sand and not cigarette ends, the water buckets are filled with water at all times and firefighting equipment on the stand is in working order. The Company Commander will see you at 1500hrs this afternoon and the QMSI of the Army Physical Training Corps will see you in his office in the gymnasium at 0900hrs tomorrow ; don't be late.'

The task ahead looked daunting but it was an opportunity to prove that I was worthy of my chevrons. Handling the members of the staff was a daunting proposition but I welcomed the challenge, I think.

'Welcome back Cpl. Gee,' said Major Philipson, 'I presume that you had a good leave and are now ready to join the staff of L Company.'

'Yes sir.' I answered confidently.

'I'm sure that you will enjoy life in the gymnasium and QMSI Robinson will keep me in the picture. You should go along to the stores now and draw up your PT kit. The Company Sergeant Major has liaised with the Company Quarter Master Sergeant for your kit to be ready. You have a lot to do over the next 24 hours; good luck Cpl Gee. Company Sergeant Major march him out.'

My head was spinning and I decided to go over to the Corporal's Mess which was a large room off the cookhouse and scrounge a mug of tea, take it back to my room, make a private little corner for myself and sort out my bed space and my kit. Although the cooks were all busy in the kitchen, the sergeant made a hot, fresh pot of tea and took time out to share it with me. I think the new chevrons on my arm made all the difference and a friendly chat at that moment perked me up.

That evening, I introduced myself to the staff of both rooms although word had spread that there was a new L/Cpl I/C the rooms. Some already knew me from before Christmas when the Company won the boxing and I had been in the team. I sensed that there was some resentment to me being 18 years of age just out of training and placed in charge of them but I was prepared to deal with that and made it clear in a friendly way that I had been given the responsibility of the NCO I/C staff and accommodation and I would carry it out to the best of my ability. I told them that if I could, I would help them with any problems that they might have but I expected their support and co-operation in carrying out my duties and responsibilities. Heads were nodded in agreement and my approach and tactics seemed to go down well but time would tell.

I drew up from the stores my PT vests, red and black striped jersey, red belt, PT shoes which had to be blackened that evening and blue serge trousers which the L/Sgt in the tailor's shop adjusted the waist and length to fit my measurements within half an hour. After breakfast the following morning, I made my way up the hill to the two very large buildings which were the gymnasiums where I was met by Sgt Instructor MacRitchie APTC. He introduced me to the regimental

Assistant Physical Training Staff; twelve in all from the five regiments of Foot Guards who were lined up to meet me. 'You know of course L/Cpl Morton Scots Guards has been posted to his battalion and has been replaced by L/Cpl Moffat.' he said. 'You will work with him and he will keep you right until you find your feet but I know all the instructors will advise and help you settle in. They are a good bunch and we all work as a team.'

'Thank-you Staff.' I said.

'Right come away into the office and meet the boss.'

QMSI Robinson wore a white physical training pullover with the APTC badge sitting in the centre. He had a large chest and broad shoulders, a round face with a pleasant smile which matched his warm welcoming handshake. During an informal chat, he asked where I was from, about my background and why I would like to join the PT Staff. He informed me about gymnasium cleaning, Staff Parade and Inspection every morning at 0815hrs. He spoke of reading and keeping up to date with the Weekly Training Programme, preparation of lessons, ensuring that the appropriate dress was worn for the particular lesson to be taught eg. gymnasia work, battle training, assault course, or sports. 'Punctuality, reliability, efficiency and teamwork are very important,' he said, 'and to receive respect you have to give respect. Work hard, enjoy your work, and feel free to speak to me at any time if you have a problem, a personal worry or want a confidential chat. Your company will expect you to carry out regimental duties which is all part of your training towards becoming a good NCO but you must let me know in plenty time when those duties arise. I have applied for you to attend a three week Preliminary Physical Training Course at the Eastern Command School of Physical Training at Shorncliffe in Kent commencing in May. If you are successful in passing, you will go directly on to the Army School of Physical Training in Aldershot for a three month Assistant Physical Training Course. The other instructors who have already been to Aldershot and passed their courses will brief you and help you in your preparation but you must get yourself extremely fit. Start learning immediately the methods of leadership and how to demonstrate and instruct your lessons. Have you any questions or is there anything you would like to discuss with me at the moment?'

'No sir, thank-you.'

'You have already met Staff MacRitchie who will help you with any difficulties that may arise and I look forward to having you on my staff. Perhaps you could report back after lunch and make a start.'

That afternoon, I started working in the gymnasium and began learning how to teach and instruct skills in physical training and combat fitness that I had so recently been through myself as a recruit. The instructors took me in hand and I understudied classes regardless of the regiment although I sometimes found it difficult to understand the Irish and Welsh accents when the instructors were speaking quickly but I could follow their demonstrations and understand the reactions of the recruits. Through rope climbing, circuit training, vaulting and agility to assault course, high aerial tree walks and rope bridges, self-defence, crossing water hazards wearing full equipment, lifting and carrying assimilated wounded comrades and all the various running tests and sports that took place in and around the Training Battalion, recent memories came flooding back. I was now learning to demonstrate exercises, assist with catching bodies that hurtled over the vaulting horses at all sorts of angles and coach in the techniques being used. I became aware of the safety aspects of the numerous and varied activities taking place; dealing with the inevitable bumps and knocks that occurred whilst encouraging co-ordination, speed and skills through teamwork, for example, in getting over the 12 foot wall.

On our morning break as we sat around the large coal burning stove in the staff room next to the office, eating our steak pies which someone had taken orders for and fetched from the NAAFI, we laughed and joked about recent occurrences within the regiments and gymnasium life. Whilst the January weather was freezing, blowing blizzards and even snowing outside, I was enjoying my new found niche in life and I was fitting in with the ways of the PT Staff, but the daily regimental responsibilities that I had within L Company was another matter.

One Friday night or rather into the wee hours of Saturday morning when lights out had been sounded, all was quiet and peaceful except for various pitches of snoring reverberating around the staff room when the door burst open and a figure staggered down the centre of the room and fell on to the second last bed from the right. All was quiet until approximately 25 minutes later the door flew open again and another figure shouting and cursing stormed through, ignoring calls to be quiet and to close the room door. He halted at the same bed space as the previous incumbent, leaned over and hauled Guardsman Smith by the collar off his bed.

'I'll teach you to bribe my girl into having sex with you.' shouted Guardsman Brian Hill as he whacked Smith on the jaw.

I jumped out of bed but by the time I had reached the light switch, the two of them were rolling around on the floor in a wild frenzy with arms and legs flailing in all directions, shouting and swearing at each other.

'She didn't need much persuasion, the dirty little slut. A couple of quid is hardly a bribe.' slurred Smith as he was sick all over Hill who untangled himself from the brawl and was trying to stand up when Smith picked up a nearby chair and crashed it down on him. Both were now smelling strongly of alcohol and vomit and were trying to stay on their feet as they slid around on the foul smelling pool of yellow and green liquid.

By this time others had jumped out of bed and grabbed the pair of them; keeping them apart.

'Right,' I said trying to decide how to handle the situation which had to be dealt with quickly before it got worse. 'Smith, get dressed. I don't know the full story but both of you are drunk, incapable of controlling yourselves and behaving as Guardsmen should behave and I have decided to place you both under arrest and lock you both up in the guardroom for the night. You have one minute to lock up your personal belongings and mop up this foul mess from the floor; Macdonald fetch a mop and a bucket of water.'

'But Corporal.'

'Don't argue MacDonald, get the mop and bucket or you will be joining these two in the guardroom.'

'Yes Corporal,' replied MacDonald who quickly realised that I wasn't in the mood for discussing the matter.

'Hay, Stevens and you Martin get dressed quickly. You are to escort the prisoners under my charge to the guardroom. Rudd you get over and warn the Sergeant of the Guard that I am bringing two prisoners to the guardroom and ask if he would please prepare two cells. Robertson, open up some windows and let in some fresh air.'

'Hill and Smith I'm charging you both with being drunk and disorderly accompanied by aggressive behaviour and bodily contact aimed at injuring one another.'

I wasn't sure that the wording was correct but I had to diffuse the situation and would deal with the report and the official charge later. Sergeant Oliver Coldstream Guards who was on duty as Sergeant of the Guard was very helpful and assisted me in completing the charge sheet and advising me on the wording for giving my verbal evidence the following morning when the two prisoners would appear in front of the Company Commander prior to attending the Commanding Officer's Orders.

It was decided that both were at fault, there had been no serious injuries, the incident was contained within the barrack room and apologies were extended to each other with a promise to amicably resolve the matter as far as the girl was concerned. They were awarded three Extra Staff Drills on consecutive Wednesday afternoons wearing full kit and equipment, two weekends of fatigues in the Sergeant's Mess and a reduction of their pay for one month; the incident to be recorded on their Conduct Sheets.

In Addition to gymnasium duties, regimental duties had to be carried out as per rota systems. Guard duties were based overnight in the guardroom, inspection of the cleanliness of accommodation, bed spaces and lockers was daily; Duty Messing (Cookhouse) NCO involved monitoring meals and listening to and recording complaints. Spot checks after reveille were carried out to ensure that no one was still lying in bed and Duty NCO NAAFI involved ensuring disciplined behaviour during bar hours and the clearing of premises after closing time. Listening to and resolving occurring problems within the staff rooms and sometimes having to report them to the CSM was an ongoing task. Charging and giving evidence as required against members of staff who failed to obey orders as given, either verbally or written down was often unpleasant but necessary along with the other duties as required of a Lance Corporal trying to prove that he was worthy of his rank and ready for promotion in the future.

As each week passed, my self-confidence grew and I felt that the attitude of the staff room was beginning to warm towards me; I was getting respect, support and assistance in carrying out my regimental duties. I was enjoying my physical training work and every day I was learning something new whilst having fun and a laugh with my new friends and colleagues. As May approached, I was very much looking forward to heading to Shorncliffe and hopefully on to Aldershot to complete my Instructor's Course. On the day of my departure all the lads shook my hand, made humorous comments and wished me luck. I was now on my way to an experience that I could never have dreamed of when I left home to join the Scots Guards.

In March 1960 ''L'' Company Scots Guards disbanded and became ''K'' Company The Guards Depot which had relocated from Caterham to Pirbright shortly afterwards.

Chapter 16 - Shorncliffe

Sixteen students including myself formed up as Course 72B on the Preliminary PT Course at the Eastern Command School of Physical Training at Shorncliffe near Folkestone in Kent. The School was under the command of Captain (Master at Arms) Victor Hugo who was about to be posted to the ASPT Aldershot. SMI (Wo1) Barwell and three APTC Instructors made up the other members of staff.

The students were from all different regiments in the British Army and although I was the only one from a Guards Infantry Regiment there was one lad from the Lifeguards. I somehow knew that when we lined up for the section photograph dressed in our red and black striped jerseys that I felt at ease and was going to enjoy the three week course and hopefully be selected to go on to Aldershot.

The accommodation was a system of wooden huts known as spiders and the living and sleeping accommodation was linked by corridors to washrooms, showers, toilets and a large drying room where wet clothing could be hung up; all were shared by the students attending the various sports and recreational courses being run at the School. The facilities were kept warm by a central heating system of radiators and there was always plenty of hot water after daily activities for showers and baths which were cleaned along with the toilets by civilian cleaners. With the daily routine of fitness exercises and physical exertion, meals were a very important part of each day; the quality of food and the self-help system was appreciated by all students.

Our course was divided into teams with different team leaders nominated each day who would produce a training programme and carry out the exercises which were based on the tables in the pamphlets issued to us. The programme was carried out under the auspices of the Instructors who after each lesson would discuss with their teams, the qualities of the leadership shown by the

137

team leader, the work rate and enjoyment of the class, the progression and safety aspect of the training and the demonstration of activities. The preparation, planning, layout and the inspection of the ropes, mats, beams, vaulting horses and all equipment was important before being used daily. After lunch, the programme continued until 1630hrs allowing time for showers and changing into smart casual wear before the evening meal.

The daily programme was intense and devised to teach leadership qualities, agility, co-ordination, strength, and dexterity, stamina, climbing, balancing and vaulting skills, jumping, running, assault course, safety in all aspects and teamwork. The evenings were spent cleaning, washing, ironing our kit and preparing our lesson for the following morning before retiring to the NAAFI for a couple of beers, a blether and a game of dominoes. The spirits were high on the course and the atmosphere in the accommodation was good but because of the nature of the course most of the students were ready to retire to bed fairly early. Although we were all Junior NCOs, which was a requirement of attending the course, there was no Corporals Mess and all students attending courses shared meals in the cookhouse and use of the NAAFI in the evenings. The Army Boxing, Basketball and Athletic Teams were using allocated accommodation whilst training for oncoming competitions. With various army units and their families in the area, Folkestone which was on our doorstep was a lively and popular town.

The days passed quickly and it was unfortunate when Craig Martin Royal Engineers slipped and fell off a log whilst traversing a ditch; he twisted his knee and had to be Returned To Unit (RTU) but was told that he would be welcomed back on the next course or when he had regained his fitness. Will Brown from the Anglian Regiment also had to leave the course for compassionate reasons of a death in the family but he too would return on the next available course. Everyone was desperately hoping to pass the course.

Each day was hectic physically and mentally but we were fit and had the energy that our bodies and minds called for. When we were told that a dance was to be held in the NAAFI on Friday evening, we all agreed that it would be a bit of fun and an opportunity to relax with some refreshments to end the week. A notice on the Information Board read that all courses and members of various named smaller units stationed nearby would be welcomed by the organising committee if they wished to attend. Local girls were to be invited and a bus would be laid on to transport them to and from the dance. Our course was warned by the staff not to get into any trouble that would jeopardise our future careers.

On that Friday afternoon, the programme ran as normal but we were called into the office one at a time to discuss with the SMI, what we felt that we had achieved on the course so far and how he and the staff thought we were progressing with one week to go. At 1500hrs all sections moved into the gymnasium where benches had been laid out for an informal chat with the Commandant, the SMI and the instructors. The Master at Arms who was dressed in uniform had a row of campaign ribbons on his left breast, laid his hat and cane down on the lectern and smiled which accentuated the scar on his left cheek. The rumour was that he had received it from a sabre cut during an army fencing competition. 'Well,' he said, 'I hope that you are all enjoying the course and will continue to work hard and prove to be a credit to your regiments. I'm sorry that two students have had to return to their units early but I have no doubt that I will be seeing them again in the near future. I will speak to you before the course ends next week and if you have no questions, I will hand you back to Mr Barwell.'

'Sit up.' shouted the SMI as the Commandant left the room and as one we sat up, backs straight and hands by our sides until the command of 'sit easy' was given.

'Now then,' said the SMI, 'you all know your strengths and weaknesses from our meeting this afternoon. You have one week to convince me and my Staff Instructors that you are worthy of a place on the Assistant Physical Training Course at Aldershot. At present the instructors have informed me that you are working hard but some of you who have been given stripes for the course are lacking a little bit in your assertiveness and leadership and one or two of you are not as physically fit as you should be. You have one week to book that seat on the train for Aldershot. Roberts are you alright?' he asked suddenly. 'Your eyes are sticking out like chapel hat pegs.'

'I'm fine sir.' was the reply.

'I bet you were thinking about the dance to-night. Well let me just warn you all to keep out of trouble, no punch ups with lads from the other units and don't be led astray by the girls or you will never even be considered for a seat on the train. Do I make myself clear?'

'Yes sir.' we replied.

'Right, get the gymnasium floor swept, wall bars dusted, all the equipment put away and everything left tidy for Monday morning, and on a satisfactory inspection by your instructors, you will be free to go a bit earlier which will help all of you who are going off for the weekend. Those who are staying, I hope you enjoy the dance, don't drink too much, keep out of trouble and I'll see you all sharp on Monday morning.'

'Thank-you sir.' and with an energetic flurry, the work was completed and we headed back to the accommodation for showers before tea. Three or four of the lads who were stationed or lived in army married quarters in Kent, packed a rucksack or a holdall and with a shout and a wave were off and away for the week-end.

That night the NAFFI was heaving with customers. The sound and noise from the band seemed to vibrate off the walls and shake the dance floor which was packed with gyrating bodies. The two bars were doing a roaring trade and after managing to get a round of beers in, five of us somehow got a table and some chairs in an adjacent room normally used for quiet chats and reading; no chance of that tonight, I thought to myself but at least we could relax over a cold lager, glimpse the talent, have a good laugh and enjoy the night. As the evening rolled by we all ordered hamburgers and chips and by the time we had a few more ales and been to the gents umpteen times, chatted to some lads attending other courses, we looked at each other in amazement and checked our watches as a voice announced, 'take your partners for the last dance.' It was nearly 0100hrs.

'Let's have one for the road.' someone suggested.

'Better hurry up then before the bars closes.' said Walter Greenfield

'My round.' said John Thomson as he stood up and headed for the bar.

I'll give you a hand.' I said picking up the tray from where it had lain against the wall since the last round. The dancing ended and the building began to empty but as we had a free day tomorrow, we were in no hurry to finish our drinks and by the time we went outside, the bus that had brought the girls had left with any taxies that had been called and most had gone home for the night.

'There were a few empty seats on that bus.' remarked Jock Malone who had popped outside to see if there were any girls looking for an escort home.

'No luck?' asked Barney.

'Naw,' replied Jock, they must have walked, or jumped into a taxi.'

'Or staying the night.' said Barney Green. We all looked at each other and laughed.

We reached our room, switched on the light and as we passed Mike Mitchell's bed, John made some remark about Mike sleeping at the bottom of his bed and suddenly having a fine mop of long curly red hair.

'Mike's away for the week-end.' I said.

'Well,' said Jock in his strong Glaswegian accent, 'somebody's not only sleeping at the bottom of his bed but somebody else is at the top!' and it was then that two girls sat up at either end of the bed and scowled at us.

'Would you stop talking and get that light off. We're trying to get some sleep.' shouted the one with her head on the pillow at the top of the bed.

'I don't think you should be in that bed.' I said.

'Taffy Roberts who has gone home with our best friend brought us in here when we missed the bus. He said, we could have this spare bed for the night as long as we were up and out by 7am before the Orderly Officer came around and we were not to tell anyone that he said it was alright.'

'Right that's fine,' said Walter, 'don't forget to pick your clothes up off the floor and put them on before you leave. It will be cold in the morning.'

'Don't be cheeky now,' said the one at the bottom of the bed, 'or we'll report you to Taffy, he's a Colonel you know.'

'We looked at each other and burst out laughing. 'Sorry, we didn't know.' I said.

'In case we have to relieve ourselves during the night, where do we find the ladies toilets?' asked the one at the bottom of the bed.

'There are no ladies' toilets in here and I wouldn't go wandering through those long dark corridors in the middle of the night.' replied Walter.

'What do you suggest then?' she asked. 'The window sill looks a bit high to hang out and over and we'd hate to get midge bites.'

'You could use the fire buckets.' suggested John pointing in their direction. 'I think they need filled anyway.' We all nodded in agreement conjuring up pictures in our own minds.

'Thankyou,' she said. 'Colonel Taffy said that you were all gentlemen in this room.'

'Well in that case,' said Barney, 'lights off gents before we strip in front of the girls, pyjamas on and into

142

bed and we'll let the girls get back to sleep unless they want to tuck us all in first.'

'No chance.' was the reply. 'Do you think I'm your mother?' Two minutes later there was loud snoring emanating from both ends of that bed.

It was the early hours of the morning when two shadows tip-toed past my bed towards the door which creaked open and closed again.

'They've gone.' muttered John who was first up that morning and had a hint of disappointment in his voice.

'Well they've left something behind.' said Walter, pointing to a pair of white pants lying stretched out on the bottom of the bed with the letters 'Ta!' printed on them.

Later that morning when Taffy crept in and was asked if Mike knew that his bed had been occupied and kept warm all night, all he could say was that he felt obliged to help a couple of damsels in distress when they had missed their bus and he was sure that Mike would have agreed.

'Och! that's fine then.' said Jock as we laughed and headed to the cookhouse for breakfast, glancing down to see if the fire buckets had been filled during the night and they had.

On the last week of the course, we were tested on our leadership qualities, marked on our written exams and scored on our physical ability and prowess in vaulting and agility, participation in games and potted sports and the quality of our individual skills and teamwork. The three weeks had passed very quickly and it was with trepidation on the Friday morning that we again entered the office to be informed of our results by Captain Hugo. Unfortunately one lad was not ready to go but the rest of us had passed and travel warrants had been arranged for us.

After a further briefing by the SMI, all the staff wished us good luck with our progress in physical training. We thanked them for the course that we had all enjoyed and shook hands with them.

On Monday morning, everyone was aboard the train heading for Aldershot, the Ancestral Home of the British Army.

Chapter 17 - Aldershot

It was early June in 1960 when we stepped from the station into a warm Aldershot sunny afternoon. As our kit was loaded on to a three tonner army vehicle, we clambered aboard the other two waiting to take us through the bustling main Street, down Queens Avenue, past the Army School of Physical Training and into Hammersley Barracks, our home for the next three months.

We were divided into nominated sections with allocated rooms as listed on the general notice board. I was in number 3 section of No. 73 Assistant Instructors Course based on the first floor of the barrack block which at first glance seemed a bit run down. Rumours from Shorncliffe were that the buildings were to be completely renovated in the near future, including the sleeping accommodation, toilets and showers. There were fourteen students in the section under SSI (S/Sgt Instructor) John Baker and SI (Sgt Instructor) Terry Hellicar who had recently passed with his course of Probationary Students into the Corps. Each section had a nominated leader who had the responsibility of ensuring that all duties when listed were carried out and that discipline prevailed within the section.

When we had reported to the Quartermaster's stores, drawn up our bedding, selected and sorted out a locker and bed space which I managed to earmark by a window, all four sections met their instructors and were given a general briefing about the course.

After lunch we were given a tour of the PT School and like all students before us, we stood in awe inside the renowned Fox Gymnasium and looked up at the large sign bearing the Cross Swords with Crown above and the words below 'MENS SANA IN CORPORE SANO' which means (Healthy Mind And Healthy Body). The gymnasium was huge and filled with all the physical training equipment that you could possibly imagine. The Museum was upstairs and from the adjoining balcony, we looked down on to a myriad of coloured lines marked out on the floor which facilitated the numerous sports, games and fun activities that could be played; basketball, badminton, volleyball, indoor soccer, circuit training and relay races were but a few. Equipment required for normal physical training leadership classes such as ropes and beams were off to the sides of the floor and operated by pulleys whilst gymnastic and judo mats, vaulting horses, and other training equipment were tucked away at either end of the gymnasium along with the Display High Horse and gymnastic safety crash mats, but all were easily accessible.

Facilities included the staff changing and locker room, showers, rest room where members of the staff could write up or amend their daily training programmes on one side of the gymnasium with student's changing rooms, showers, toilets and First Aid Room on the other.

Napier Room (meetings, briefings and lectures), Brown Gym (gymnastics) and Henslow Room (fencing) were outside and adjacent to Fox Gym. There were offices for the Commandant, Chief Instructor, Staff Officers, Admin and Pay staff as well as an office for the Secretary, Major (retd) Tom Fletcher of the Corps Association and the RSM. To reach the Wand-Tetley Gymnasium which upstairs housed the Boxing Room complete with a full size ring, one passed the Officer's Coffee Room and the Student's NAFFI.

The assault course and confidence area containing the death slide were designed to develop courage, balance, determination, skill and a will to overcome any inner fears that students might have had when taking part in those testing activities. Various forms of swimming, lifesaving, diving, water polo and sub aqua were taught in the Command Baths under the guidance of Tom Kennedy an ex APTC Instructor and a well-known and respected gentleman around the world of Aldershot and swimming.

Locking up and securing the premises after evening activities which went on to approximately 2200 hours was a major responsibility for duty instructors who carried out the role of Orderly Sergeants and Orderly Officers/Warrant Officers. Having the correct keys for the correct lock and knowing the whereabouts of every light switch was a daunting task along with remembering which outside security light had to be left on. For purposes of morning cleaning by students, all facilities had to be opened early and again duty staff had to have early breakfasts, collect keys from the guardroom and ensure that all was ready for the morning staff briefings and student's parade taken by the RSM and The Training Warrant Officer.

Situated next to the School was the Army Athletic, Football and Rugby Stadium and across the Queens Avenue lay the large expanse of open plan sports fields known as the Polo Fields; used for football, rugby, running, jogging, walking, multi-purpose training and various activities by military and civilians alike. Areas were roped off to allow Freefall Parachutists Display Teams to practice landing and some folks just enjoyed exercising their dogs or pushing buggies or prams while their little ones enjoyed the fresh air.

A very short distance away was Mons Officer Cadet School which trained civilians, many from abroad, for Short Service Commissions whilst a few miles up the road at Camberley resplendent in its magnificent building and grounds sat the Royal Military Academy of Sandhurst where young well educated men were trained and passed into army regiments throughout the world serving with Regular Commissions.

RSM Howard briefed us on how the early morning cleaning was to be carried out and warned us that all students would be involved. Sections would be allocated areas of work which included indoor facilities where students had to march up and down in a line wielding large brooms and mops on the main floors whilst wall bars and equipment were dusted down. Outdoor areas were to be checked, swept and cleaned as necessary. We were informed that we were to march in sections to

147

and from Hammersley Barracks daily ensuring that we had enough time to finish all duties prior to the morning parade. He covered all matters of duties, discipline, cleanliness, inspections and any problems that might arise. He spoke of hilarity being controlled in the NAFFI, expectations from Junior NCOs and students on the course and general standards of conduct. 'Work hard and you will ensure that you are a credit to your regiments and that you do enjoy the course.' he emphasised. 'I will now pass you over to Major Grieve the Chief Instructor who wishes to say a few words.'

'Good morning gentlemen.' said Major Grieve, a short stocky man from the Duke of Wellington's Regiment, 'The Commandant Lt. Col Lucas, MC will address you all tomorrow. I will not repeat all that the RSM has briefed you on but I wish to welcome you and inform you of one or two extremely important events which you will be involved in very shortly.'

'As you may well know, 1960 is the Centenary Year, 1860-1960 of The Army Physical Training Corps and on Saturday, 18th June The Colonel Commandant, Field-Marshal The Viscount Montgomery of Alamein, K.G., G.C.B., D.S.O. will be accepting The Freedom Of The Borough Of Aldershot on behalf of the Army Physical Training Corps from The Mayor of Aldershot, Councillor G. A. North, J.P.'

'You will be involved in a variety of duties including assisting with the laying out and retrieving the equipment for the Corps Gymnastic Display Team on the day and throughout the summer months at various fetes. Full details of your involvement will be disclosed later. This Celebratory Year will end on the 8th December when a Cavalcade Of Physical Training will be held here at the School and again some of you will be involved with the proceedings.'

'To accommodate the above, your Assistant Physical Training Course is slightly longer than normal and will be enhanced by these memorable events. You are fortunate to be part of the making of APTC History. Your

148

units have been informed and have agreed to the extended time of the course; you will report back to your units at the termination of the course.'

There were no questions from the floor but the atmosphere was buzzing and we couldn't wait to get started. The Morning Parade in Fox Gymnasium was taken by the RSM and all students had to attend; Officer's courses, specialist sports courses in gymnastics, boxing, basketball and fencing to name but a few; Assistant Instructors, Advance, Probationer and the APTC Refresher Courses with their relevant instructors were all present. Roll call was taken and various sections were inspected by the Duty Staff Officer. Details were given out by course instructors and queries answered before the first lessons commenced, which for Assistant Instructor's courses, were warm up exercises in their sections. The leadership qualities of individual students were discussed with marks scored for planning and preparation, layout of equipment, demonstrations, teaching, coaching and encouragement given to other students.

The Training Programme was hectic from morning until late afternoon when we marched back in our sections down Queens Avenue to our accommodation for showers before tea unless we were going back to the gymnasium in the evening for extra practice on such as vaulting and agility or groundwork and tumbling on the mats prior to weekly testing.

Saturday morning was a relief and those who couldn't make it home for the week-end packed a holdall with dirty washing and headed for the near bye busy laundrettes. Aldershot was a hive of activity at any time but a Saturday morning was always extremely busy with squaddies making use of their free time to do some shopping, collect their necessities, have a few beers, a good laugh and enjoy life with their comrades before being whisked off on army duties somewhere in the world.

The market in the centre of town was very popular with soldiers and their families purchasing at cheap prices everything from groceries, toiletries and clothes to toys, tools and DIY gadgets; The owner of the huge butcher's van was a character and his style of jokes, vocabulary and cockney accent pulled in the crowds as he auctioned the hams, poultry and varieties of meats for his give a way prices as he called them.

Although most soldiers preferred to wear casual civilian clothes at weekends, some because of duties or commitments had to wear uniform and cap badges worn in the many coloured berets and hats distinguished the numerous regiments present. There were the famous red berets of the Parachute Regiment and Airborne Units with their camouflaged smocks, the standard dark blue berets worn by some regiments or the light blue of the Army Air Corps; green of the Intelligence Corps and Light Infantry or brown of the Hussars; Glengarries and Tam O Shanters of the Scottish Regiments and many other forms of dress worn by soldiers who were often stationed far afield but were attending courses in the area.

The Queen Alexandria Royal Army Nursing Corps and Royal Army Medical Corps staffed the hospital and the adjacent busy Princess Louise Margaret Maternity Wing which was kept busy with wives and their new born babies. Regiments and Corps that frequented Aldershot were numerous including the Royal Army Dental Corps which ensured the quality of the gums and teeth of soldiers and their families and the WRAC which was continuously being employed in areas that had previously been considered the male domain. Rows of horses were daily exercised in pairs to and from the Cavalry Barracks and were cared for by the Royal Army Veterinary Corps not to mention the polo and gymkhana ponies that entertained the large crowds who turned up to watch at various spectacles throughout the area.

The NAFFI CLUB was a popular meeting place for refreshments, meals and Saturday night dancing but along with local pubs, dance halls and cinemas often attracted (especially after a few beers) over friendly girls and late night punch ups for which the Military Police nicknamed The Redcaps were usually on hand to deal with. It was wise to stay well clear of these establishments especially on Saturday nights and we did; preferring to go back to our barracks for lunch and afterwards, attend one of the many rugby or other sporting events taking place in the area, including Aldershot Town if playing football at home. It paid off to get down to the laundrettes early on Saturday mornings and was worth the extra shilling to leave the clothes to be washed, aired and dried by the attendant and collected later by ourselves, leaving us time to relax and enjoy a frothy coffee with a bacon roll, have a bit of banter, do some shopping and discuss the happenings of the week.

Sunday was generally a day of relaxation, catching up with ironing, strolling across the Polo Fields where there was always activities to watch. Homework and preparing lessons for Monday were always to be considered; oh!, and watching television in the NAFFI in the evening unless of course, I was on duty with others in the guardroom.

The days rolled by quickly and the 18th June had suddenly arrived. The day was dry and sunny and at 1445hrs The Band of the1st Battalion The Parachute Regiment marched into the Recreation Ground and played a Medley of Old Songs during the assembly of spectators. At 1500hrs three companies of Warrant Officers and Non-Commissioned Officers under the Officer Commanding the Parade, Lt. Col. C.W.V. Hankinson OBE. marched on as the band played The Standard of St. George.

After The Mayor and the Colonel Commandant reviewed the parade and the Chaplains said prayers, a number of formal proceedings took place in which the Colonel Commandant accepted the invitation from the Mayor to sign the roll of Honorary Freemen on behalf of the Corps and accepted the scroll and the casket designed specifically to contain the scroll.

At 1545 hrs, the Mayor and the Colonel Commandant took the salute as the parade marched past in column of route to the APTC MARCH which was followed by a review of the Old Comrades of the Corps while the band played 'Boys of the Old Brigade'. This was followed by rapturous applause as the Gymnastic Display Team ran in to the centre of the arena and gave a wonderful display of artistic and gymnastic skills. At the end of the display the parade formed up and advanced in review order to give a General Salute followed by The National Anthem.

At 1625 hrs the parade accompanied by the band commenced its march through a packed Aldershot to Salamanca Barracks with drums beating and bayonets fixed. It was a great day for all members, past members of the corps, associated members and all their families. It was a very moving experience and the memory has never left me; little did I know that **over 50 years later** I would be marching through Aldershot town centre with the **Royal** Army Physical Training Corps exercising their right to the Freedom of the Borough of Rushmoor in celebration of the **'Royal' Title on Saturday the 17th Sep 2011.** I was so pleased and proud to share that moment with Carmine who had accompanied me to Aldershot.

The course was hectic and hard work but I loved every moment of it and I had made many new friends as well as improving my confidence and ability in communicating with other Junior Non Commissioned Officers. Like all the other students, I shrugged off bumps, knocks and bruises with help and guidance from the Medical Sergeant who supplied the elastoplasts, muscle rub and support strapping for the joints as required. As a member of No.3 Section of the 73 Assistant Instructors Course, I was so pleased to step forward and accept a certificate for being a member of the team that won the Inter-Section Flag Competition.

On the 22nd June to the 9th July, the Corps gave a Centenary Commemoration Display (High Horse Vaulting Gymnastic Display) at the Royal Tournament at Earls Court, London.

On the16th September there was a Centenary Commemoration Ball followed by a Centenary Reunion Dinner on the 17th September at the ASPT which we assisted with the work involved.

The course came to an end; I had passed and been recommended to return for the Advance Course which was the gateway to being selected into the Army Physical Training Corps. I said farewell to all my new friends some of which I was destined to see again in the future.

On the 8th December, as part of the Centenary Celebrations the annual Assault-At-Arms had been replaced by a Centenary (1860-1960) Cavalcade of Physical Training held at the ASPT. I had put my name down as a volunteer to assist if my unit would allow me to attend and stay for two days which they did. Once again Field- Marshal Montgomery who had been Colonel Commandant of the Corps since1946 would be in attendance with The Inspector of Physical Training, Brigadier A.E.C. Bredin D.S.O, M.C. and The Commandant of the ASPT Lt. Col. Lucas. What a gathering it turned out to be.

After a very entertaining evening and some highly polished displays of fencing, trampolining and gymnastics, the High Vaulting Horse Display team gave a stirring performance to a rapturous applause by the audience; after the formalities, a dinner with speeches finished a very memorable evening and a worthwhile experience for me.

When I had reported back at the end of my Assistant Instructors Course to the Guards Depot which was now at Pirbright, the CSM informed me that I was to move into a bunk and share it with Bob Crosby a fellow L/Cpl who was a drill instructor. I was no longer in charge of the Staff Room and had to concentrate on my work in

Physical Training. Wow!! I couldn't believe it; fantastic! Bob was already living in the room and I was given the top bunk bed which suited me fine; he made me very welcome and said he would show me all the tricks in cleaning white belts and buffing up boots for duties if I would help him stay fit and keep his weight down; we both agreed and got on well together.

I settled into life very quickly and felt proud to be an Assistant Physical Training Instructor in the Scots Guards. Christmas was almost on us and as snow fell on the 10th of December I celebrated my 19th birthday in the Corporal's Mess with the lads and a lot of beer. Two weeks later, my 14 days leave pass was signed and I felt good to be heading home to Edinburgh again, and Carmine.

.

Chapter18 - Wedding Plans

It was great to be home again with Carmine and our families over Christmas. We enjoyed New Year which as usual rolled into a number of musical evenings with dad on the piano, and ourselves and the neighbours singing heartily with plenty of food and drink on the table. It was now January 1961 and time for Carmine and me to sit down and plan our big day.

After much discussion we thought about getting married in St Marys Episcopalian Cathedral in Palmerston Place near Grove Street where I grew up as a boy and had attended Sunday School with my younger brother Ally. The costs were a bit too much and it seemed at the time, all a bit pompous; we weren't sure that it was what we really wanted.

We had already agreed that although Carmine was Catholic and I was Protestant, we were not going to let religion stand in our way; after all we were both Christian with strong principals of right and wrong and good and bad. After a long discussion, we arranged to meet the local priest with a view to getting married in the chapel of Saint Columbus at Salisbury and I spent some time discussing issues such as birth control and a variety of matters with him and although I was very happy to promise to bring our children up as Christians, I could not promise God to bring them up in the Catholic faith; preferring to allow them and ourselves the freedom of choice as they grew up.

We now decided to take our vows in the Registrar Office in the Tron Square in Edinburgh and set the date for the 22nd April 1961. We agreed that Carmine would ask Margaret Cooper her best friend from school to be her Best Maid and I would ask Colin Downham, a member of the Scots Guards physical training staff at Pirbright and a very good friend of mine to be our Best Man. After checking our financial position and seeking various quotes, we decided that our reception would be held in the Clifton Rooms in Lauriston Place near the

Edinburgh Royal Infirmary with the catering to be carried out by St. Cuthbert's Co-operative. Details of cars, band, invitations, menu, speeches and more importantly, where we were going to live were all discussed and planned as best as we could. We had now to tell our families about our selected day; we did and they were all very happy about it in spite of being a bit concerned about our ages. I was nineteen and Carmine was a very mature eighteen years of age.

Once again Carmine saw me off back to London on the train from the Waverly Station. My mind was bustling full of thoughts and it felt that I had no sooner closed my eyes when the train was pulling into Kings Cross in the wee small hours of the morning.

Granda (Charlie) Neri passed away that January and was a very sad loss to the whole family. He had travelled over from Cervaro near Monte Cassino and settled in Scotland where he met and married Maria from the Milan area of Italy. He will always be remembered for his Italian looks, large moustache, cap on his head, walking stick in his hand and his stories of the past from Italy which he so much enjoyed telling us. He made regularly the Sunday lunch of spaghetti Italian style for the family gathering and I was very fortunate to be made welcome into that world.

Life at Pirbright was hectic but I was very much enjoying it and coping with all the physical training instruction, gymnasium duties and regimental duties that as a L/Cpl I had to perform. As I was under 21years of age, I had to request permission from my Commanding Officer to get married which he gave me once I had assured him that I had considered my responsibilities and that I had been looking into renting a house in the Farnborough area where some members of the Company already lived. Because of my age I was not entitled to an army quarter or an army hiring and had the responsibility of finding suitable accommodation for Carmine and myself.

The cross country season was underway and I came second in the Depot Championships and was selected to represent the Depot Team in the London District Championship Finals where we finished third to battalion teams from the Coldstream and Scots Guards. By now the Depot Team was running regularly on Saturday afternoons in the local Cross country league usually over six and a half mile courses and we were doing well. I was also playing rugby but the Welsh Guards were too strong for most other teams around. I was boxing at Light Middle weight and winning although to win the London District Championship, I had to sweat down to Welter Weight at 10 stone 8 pounds which meant early morning runs, gymnasium training sparring in the ring under the appointed coach and some serious control over my intake of food in readiness for the weigh-in. I was now very fit and holding my weight well, although worried in case the black eye that I had just received in sparring would not be away before the wedding in spite of everyone telling me that it did enhance my looks but it was all worth it when I won the Welterweight Title.

The wedding day; **22nd April1961** was creeping closer and closer as all the lads in the gym kept reminding me. Colin had just got made up to Lance Sergeant, exchanged his two chevrons on his arms for three and moved into the Sergeant's Mess accommodation. I was very pleased for him but so disappointed that although I had been recommended for promotion, authority to wear my three stripes hadn't yet come through from the Brigade of Guards Headquarters and Records at Birdcage Walk in London, although I was still hoping that it would before the wedding. I so wanted to have three stripes sewn on to my pyjamas in time for the honeymoon. Really? Yeah!

Farquhar McCombie Scots Guards, Jim Pollock and Stan Woods, Coldstream Guards had all left the gymnasium, gone to Aldershot on the Advance Course, progressed to the Probationers Course and were selected for transfer to the APTC which gave Colin and me hope for the future as we were both selected to attend the same Advance Course in October 1961. SSI Derek Dolphin moved into the new Queen Elizabeth Barracks with the Welsh Guards and was a welcomed visitor to the Depot Gymnasium next door.

One day out of the blue a drill instructor Willie McGill of the Scots Guards and his wife Maureen offered to give Carmine and me a room in their house where they lived in Oak Road Farnborough in Surrey until we had found somewhere of our own which would also help them with their rent. I wrote to Carmine and we accepted which meant that she could join me down in Surrey after the wedding. There were quite a few instructors from the Depot living in Farnborough and cycling daily to work at Pirbright and I felt that it wouldn't take me long to regain my cycling legs again.

The Wedding Day was only a few days away when Colin and I boarded the train to Edinburgh with our No1 Dress (Blues), forage cap, white belt, white gloves and gleaming best boots, tucked neatly into our luggage. Carmine liked Colin and told me that he was a good choice of Best Man; Colin liked Margaret and thought that she was a good choice of Best Maid and our families liked everyone which meant that we all got on well together. As was the custom before the wedding Carmine had her Girls Night Out and I hit the town with the lads. To ensure that we all made the wedding on time which had been arranged for 1130am on the Saturday we had all agreed to have our last spell of freedom on the Thursday night.

After a few beers in as many different Edinburgh drinking establishments, the clock passed the midnight hour and someone in our group of about twelve decided that I should be stripped down to my underpants, tied to the railings of Princes Street Gardens on the main street and all except me thought it was a great idea. In spite of my protestations, the deed was carried out before the gang ran away and left me to face all who passed by enjoying a good laugh; no one asked if I was in any form of distress. With my hands behind my back, tied to the railings, I couldn't even hide my face but was only too glad that there were no policemen passing by nor that it wasn't a cold wet night. After what seemed like ages, the lads appeared laughing and joking with some newly acquired bottles of beer and my clothes. They untied me and we made our way into the gardens near the Scott Monument where we sat on the grass under some trees, had a good laugh, finished the beer and jumped into taxies to take us home. Although it was the early hours of Friday morning, my mother made up some bedding with quilts and blankets for three of the lads who were still in the party mood and had decided to see me home to enjoy a nightcap; Bobby Douglas, George MacDonald and Bertie Mainie slept on the living room floor that night. After a breakfast of bacon rolls and mugs of tea the following morning the lads shared a taxi home with promises to be at the Registrar Office early on Saturday morning. Colin who enjoyed himself and joined in the revelry said that he had never had a night out quite like it before and would always remember the Scottish hospitality.

When the alarm went off on Friday morning, both Colin and I agreed that we had made the right decision to have my night out on the Thursday and not the night before the wedding which was often the custom. We now had time to relax, check our kit and ensure that all was ready for Saturday morning. Colin again assured me that he had the ring safe. What more could a man ask for than a reliable Best Man

Chapter 19 - Our Special Day

The next morning 45 Peveril Terrace was buzzing with my mother organising breakfast whilst trying to organise Dad and ensure that everyone was getting dressed and ready including herself of course. Although Carmine lived across the road at 44 she was leaving from Maureen's, her sister's house at Magdalene Gardens. Maureen was a tower of strength at this time for Carmine who had lost her mother when she was very young.

Colin and I dabbed our No1 dress shoes with a damp duster and blotting paper to remove any blobs of water and gently rubbed with a dry yellow duster in small circles to bring up the shine, brushed down our Blues and forage caps, checked that our white belts were not smudged and were sitting straight around our waists, donned our white gloves and jumped into one of the cars waiting at the front door. We waved to the crowd of neighbours that had gathered with confetti at the ready and the children who were hovering for the traditional pooroot which we threw out of the car windows on to the pavement; mainly pennies and three penny pieces; an old custom which the children loved. Mum, Dad, Ally and Eleanor boarded the other car, had their pooroot and we all headed for the Tron Square.

When Carmine arrived with her dad in the Bridal Car with the white ribbons fluttering across the bonnet, I remember thinking how gorgeous she looked in her wedding dress and I think Colin was impressed with Margaret the Best Maid dressed in pink. The service went well, followed by showers of confetti from the crowd outside the Registrar Office; all the guests headed in cars and taxies for the halls. The driver took Carmine and me on a tour of Edinburgh in the Bridal Car to ensure that everyone was at the hall awaiting our arrival.

Speeches followed the meal and when Carmine's sister, Catherine from Australia had her telegram read out, 'Weather Forecast, Closer Tonight', a peal of laughter and applause went around the hall. Carmine and I were called on to the floor to lead the first dance and before long the band had everyone tripping round the floor to the Gay Gordons, Dashing White Sergeant and the Eightsome reel which, in spite of the band leader's guidance, had everyone doing their own version of the steps as well as going in all directions across the floor but laughing and enjoying the fun. A Saint Bernard's Waltz calmed things down until everyone had a go at jiving and rock and roll. Throughout, the drinks service was slick and continuous with Hearts and Hibs being a popular topic amongst the men propping up the bar.

Towards the end of the evening, Carmine changed out of her wedding dress and Colin and I changed into lounge suits. Colin was seeing Margaret home safely and staying at my mother's until the following evening when we had booked a sleeper for him to return to London. We had a great send off from the hall as the waiting taxi took us to our flat that we had rented for a few days before saying cheerio to everyone at the Waverly Station and heading on an overnight sleeper for Kings Cross and onwards to our new home in Farnborough Hampshire.

It was a lovely summer; Willie and Maureen made us very welcome and helped us to settle into married life in leafy Farnborough. I bought a second hand bike and while I cycled to work with Willie, Carmine and Maureen who was pregnant shared the housework, walked around and shopped in Farnborough.

As I was under 21 years of age, I could not apply for an army quarter or a hiring which was suitable accommodation if quarters were not available; the army paid the rent after inspection of the premises. Until the required age was reached, permission from one's Commanding Officer to marry was mandatory regardless of rank and one had to find and pay for one's own accommodation. It was all very pleasant with Willie and Maureen but when the opportunity arose to move into a near-by semi-detached house in Oak Road, we jumped at the chance and the owner a Mrs German who lived next door made us very welcome.

We bought a second hand scooter which was good fun until it fell to bits. Although I didn't have a full driver's licence, we scraped together enough to buy an old second hand banger; a Morris Minor which had an empty apple box for the front passenger seat. One Sunday afternoon we decided to go for a run down towards the shopping centre in Farnborough and as I approached a large roundabout, I tried to slow down and at the same time look to my right for oncoming traffic. I missed the brake and the car went hurtling straight up the kerb, on to the roundabout, over a large flower bed and down the kerb on the other side; talk about the Keystone Cops. We got home, parked in the drive, looked at each other and burst out laughing.

At last my promotion came through and I became a Lance Sergeant which now meant that although I had more responsibilities in the gymnasium and at the Depot, I was now a member of the Sergeant's Mess and could take Carmine to social evenings in the Mess and we could enjoy all the relevant functions including the Summer Ball. I also qualified for a most welcomed rise in pay which was paid weekly into our joint bank account and was in total £3-10 shillings. One night, we had just enough money for some shopping and were down to our last five shillings and sixpence when we decided to go and see a film in the local cinema which we did, and still had enough money left to buy a fish supper each when we came out; My pay went into the bank the following day. Happy days!!

I was now carrying out duties with more responsibilities as well as my work in the gymnasium such as Sergeant of the Guard, I/C Fire Piquet, various duties in the dining hall during meals and the Company Sergeant in Waiting which required living in the Sergeant's Mess for one week. I had to attend various drill parades and role calls, carry out personnel checks at reveille and lights out, attend Company Commander's Orders and Commandant's Memoranda as well as being on call by the senior officers of the company; I had to carry the Sergeant In Waiting's Book everywhere, entering required details such as who was sick and where staff could be found throughout the day if different to their normal place of work. All my kit and personal equipment had to be immaculate throughout the week for all parades on and off the square.

One week in the summer when I was on duty, the mess had a barbeque and I was so pleased when Carmine said that she would like to attend and could catch the bus from Farnborough on her own, and she did.

Major Philipson was still my Company Commander and had been responsible for my promotions; 'I have been impressed with your support, reliability and enthusiasm for your work within the Company.' he told me and when invited to the barbeque in the Sergeant's Mess, he asked me to introduce my wife to him. He told me afterwards it had been a privilege to meet her and I felt so proud of Carmine. He wished us both best wishes and good luck for the future. I think he liked me because I didn't make a fuss the night Bandy his boxer dog ate my steak pie which had been lying on my bed. Carmine got home safely that night with a lift in a car by Sergeant Alistair McKimmon and his wife who were also living in Farnborough.

We were enjoying the summer in Farnborough but autumn was approaching fast and I had been nominated to attend the Advance Course at the ASPT in October. I was now extremely fit and was receiving good reports for the way I carried out my military duties, the responsibilities of my rank, my general work and enthusiasm in physical training. Carmine and I talked over the implications of being selected for the APTC and agreed that although during the course, I could travel to Aldershot daily, I would have to work hard by day and get down to studying in the evening; only the top six students would be selected for the Probationers Course and be invited to transfer into the APTC. She agreed that I should try my best and to support me in every way possible.

I said farewell to all my colleagues and friends at the Depot who all wished me luck for my future and I headed for the ASPT, Aldershot in early October. There were twenty eight students on the course from various regiments stationed throughout the world including Colin; my Best Man whom I thought was an excellent candidate for the APTC. The course instructor was SSI Rod Coveney and the Officer was Major (MAA) Victor Hugo. We knew and had it confirmed on our first morning that only the top five or six would be selected for the three month Probation Course which progressed into the APTC.

Hammersley Barracks was now being refurbished and our temporary accommodation was in the old Malta Barracks which was situated across the playing fields and over the very busy Farnborough Road. Students now had to march to the ASPT under the bridge to avoid crossing the road; along the Basingstoke Canal which was muddy on wet days but everyone knew that it would be worth it when refurbishments to the original barracks were complete

The course programme consisted of intense physical participation, teaching and coaching of most sports, writing fitness training schedules for recruits and trained soldiers ensuring that units were fit to be employed in their role for war. Lecturing in appropriate subjects, examinations in the knowledge of sports and their laws / rules, Anatomy Physiology and visiting various physical education establishments and units were all covered by the programme as well as the teaching of swimming, lifesaving and close combat. We were watched, commented on and marked on how we carried out our duties and our responsibilities. We were considered as to our suitability of being Senior NCOs and a credit to the APTC if we were selected. How we dealt with difficulties that arose, solved problems and communicated with each other, personnel of all ranks including officers and privates was important and taken into consideration.

The Ministry Of Defence had just brought out an offer of two hundred pounds for all soldiers who were due to leave the army if they signed on for a further six years. My three years were up in June 1962 and I had always intended to leave the army and join the Edinburgh City Police but I would now much prefer to be selected into the APTC.

I had just celebrated my 20th birthday at home with Carmine who cooked a wonderful candlelight dinner and opened a bottle of bubbly which we shared by a warm coal fire.

At first all was very tense on the course but gradually we all started to relax, work together and help each other especially if anyone was struggling. It was a long hard three months and it was suddenly time for the course to end and the announcement to be made as to who was staying on at the ASPT after Christmas; we had all worked out whom we thought would be selected. The night before I couldn't sleep but the following morning, Carmine gave me a kiss, told me she knew that all would be well as she waved me off.

We were called in to the Commandant's Office one at a time in alphabetical order which was a dreadful experience of waiting to be told what the future held for us. It was great news for me. I had been successful with another five students. I couldn't believe it and felt as if I was walking on air. We gave our commiserations to the lads that didn't make it which included Colin and wished them all the very best for the future.

The six of us; now the new Probationers Course, drew up from the Quartermaster's stores our new APTC badges, red sashes and the relevant uniform required by sergeants of the Army Physical Training Corp in readiness for commencing on the course straight after the New Year. The course Instructor was SSI Johnny

Ions who introduced us all to the Sergeant's Mess, the rules and regulations and expected behaviour. Although I already had the experience of the Mess, I was now very happy to be a full sergeant entitled to wear the red sash.

I knew now that I would stay in the army and would have to sign on to allow me to transfer into the APTC and I did. On my way home that day, I bought Carmine a large bunch of flowers from the £200 signing on fee.

What a wonderful Christmas we had.

Chapter 20 - The Army Physical Training Corps

We now started a three month course of intense studies in a wide range of subjects appertaining to physical training but we were no longer competing for a place of acceptance into the APTC. At the end of the course, we would transfer from our regiments, be posted out to a unit somewhere in the world but would still be on a probationary period for six months during which time if we were not up to the standard required, we could be returned to our regiments; the efficient selection process meant that it very rarely happened. We all worked very hard mentally and physically and there was not an ounce of fat on us as we progressed towards the termination of the course in March 1962.

After officially transferring from our regiments, in my case the Scots Guards, to the Army Physical Training Corps we were all asked to complete a form stating where we would like to be posted to and with what type of unit eg. Infantry, Parachute Regiments, Cavalry, Army Apprentices, Royal Engineers, REME, Colleges of Mons or Sandhurst ; nothing at all was guaranteed and each posting was for approximately three years before moving on. As Carmine and I now wanted to start a family we both thought it would be a good idea if we could get a posting to Scotland to allow our son or daughter to be born there but I had done a bit of homework and knew that none of the instructors with regiments up there were due to be posted but I put it down as my first choice anyway.

'How would you like to go to a newly formed Junior Tradesmens Regiment opening up?' asked Col. (Retired) Cuerden of the Records Office at the ASPT.

'Sounds good sir. Where is it?'

'Troon in Scotland,' he said. 'There is a QMSI Dick Davis taking over the physical training programmes there and he needs a young Sergeant Instructor to assist him.'

I couldn't believe our luck and before Carmine and I knew it, we were on our way to Troon in Ayrshire. I was still not entitled to a quarter but when I telephoned the Housing Office in Dundonald Camp, they gave me details of a private hiring owned by a Mr & Mrs Guy in the town of Troon. They had available self-contained accommodation at the rear of their house in Welbeck Crescent and we took up residence in April. Carmine was now expecting our first child in September and on the 22nd Andrew James Grant Gee was born at Buckredden Maternity Hospital in nearby Irvine. Jacqueline Eleanor Gee was to follow some years later.

We had a happy time living near the sea front of Troon but on the 10th December I was 21 years of age and we moved into a quarter in the camp which had extra rooms for any of the family visiting and there was no requirement to travel to and from the gymnasiums in Dundonald Camp. My role was to operate under the guidance of Dick Davis, the fitness training programmes, recreational activities, train and coach various sporting teams in competitions throughout Scotland and to organise gymnastic displays throughout the summer months.

We had three wonderful years at Troon and when I was informed that my next posting was to HQ 48 Gurkha Infantry Brigade based in Hong Kong, Carmine and I opened a celebratory bottle of bubbly.

Before you go...

Howard's other book.

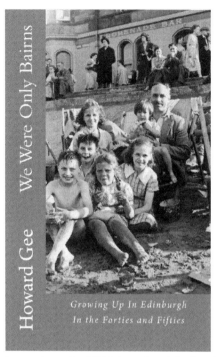

I was born in 1941 in a front facing top flat tenement building in Edinburgh within the sound of the Castle's famous One O'clock Gun. Stables at the top of the street were the main reason that horses were a regular sight; pulling carts of milk, coal, ceremonial coaches and drays from the nearby brewery but the pomp and majesty of the Household Cavalry en route to Edinburgh Castle, trotting up and down Grove Street annually during the Edinburgh Tattoo was a lasting memory for all the children who lived in or around the street. When Roy Rogers the famous cowboy, brought his even more famous horse Trigger to Edinburgh, the stable entrance was mobbed with excited children and inquisitive adults.

Printed in Great Britain
by Amazon

49989206R00102